RETIRE YOUR FAMILY KARMA

RETIRE YOUR FAMILY KARMA

Decode Your Family Pattern and Find Your Soul Path

Ashok Bedi, M.D.
Boris Matthews, Ph.D.

NICOLAS-HAYS, INC.
Berwick, Maine

First published in 2003 by
Nicolas-Hays, Inc.
P. O. Box 1126
Berwick, ME 03901-1126
www.nicolashays.com

Distributed to the trade by
Red Wheel/Weiser, LLC
P. O. Box 612
York Beach, ME 03910-0612
www.redwheelweiser.com

Note to Readers: The personal stories presented in this book are based on the authors' actual
experiences with their clients, although names have been changed to protect the clients' ano-
nymity. The information in this book is meant to provide guidelines for self-help, but psychiatric and medical conditions require help from qualified professionals. The authors and publisher
are not responsible for any action that you may take based on the information in this book.

Cataloging-in-Publication Data

Bedi, Ashok.
  Retire your family karma : decode your family pattern and find your soul path / Ashok
Bedi, Boris Matthews.
    p. cm.
Includes bibliographical references and index.
  ISBN 0-89254-081-8 (pbk. : alk. paper) 1. Self-actualization (Psychology) 2. Family--
Psychological aspects.
3. Hinduism--Psychology. 4. Karma--Psychology. I. Matthews, Boris.
II. Title.
  BF637.S4 B423 2003
  155.9'24--dc22   2003021872

Cover and book design by Kathryn Sky-Peck.

Typeset in 11/15 Adobe Garamond

TP

09 08 07 06 05 04 03

7 6 5 4 3 2 1

*The paper used in this publication meets the minimum requirements of the
American National Standard for Information Sciences—Permanence of Paper
for Printed Library Materials Z39.48–1992 (R1997).*

CONTENTS

JOURNAL EXERCISES

ACKNOWLEDGMENTS

The case examples in this book are composite cases with names and details disguised. We are privileged to be part of our patient's journeys and are grateful to them for sharing their stories to guide others on the courageous path to healing and change. Many thanks to Milwaukee Public Library for kind permission to cite their protocol for researching personal genealogy. Our special thanks to Valerie Cooper and her staff at Nicolas-Hays for their excellent suggestions.

◆　◆　◆

I WANT TO THANK MY grandparents and parents who inspired this book, my wife Usha, my daughter Ami, my son Siddhartha, my son-in-law Ralph Stayer, my grandson Signe and his mother Angela, who all bore with me during the tedious process of working on this book and generously gave me their love, encouragement, and support. I particularly want to thank my son Siddhartha, who initially helped me refine the concept of clan karma in our informal weekly father-son dinners. Finally, I wish to express a deep appreciation to my co-author, Boris, for a most enjoyable collaboration on this project and for our fellowship.

—ASHOK BEDI

WORKING WITH MY FRIEND and colleague Ashok is always an intellectually stimulating experience. Co-authoring this book with him has helped me more fully appreciate the travails and the accomplishments of my parents and grandparents, as well as of the many patients who shared their life journey with me individually and in the dream groups I have lead with my co-facilitator, Marilyn Olson. I am especially grateful to my patients who kindly permitted me to include parts of their stories and struggles. Last, but not least, I thank the many teachers who have broadened and deepened a gift first given me by my mother: an appreciation for the universality of human experience.

—BORIS MATTHEWS

◆　◆　◆

We are all faced with a positively terrifying parental backlog of repressed muck for which we are ultimately responsible as individuals, in terms of how we deal with this heritage. No one escapes. . . . Many people never heal it, and their children must then deal with the problem.

—LIZ GREENE,
The Development of the Personality (p. 160)

INTRODUCTION

Life in the West, and increasingly in the East, is lived in the fast lane. Technology is moving forward at an exponential pace. The standard of material living is gradually rising in the industrialized and developing nations. We are exploring and exploiting the treasures of Mother Earth, sometimes enhancing but more often depleting the resources for our grandchildren and future generations. As we harvest the gifts of our civilization, it is crucial that we calculate the karmic price tag. Karma is the Hindu concept of the choices we make and the consequences those choices bear. What kind of legacy are we leaving for future generations? As individuals, families, and communities, what emotional ledger sheet are we leaving for the future? Who will retire the consequences of karma we leave behind, when we leave this life with unfinished business?

In the Hindu culture, we must return as we reincarnate to finish this past life karma. However, in our clinical practice, we have learned that more often than not, it is the future generations that may reap the benefits but must also retire the karmic debt of their grandparents and ancestors. The choices we make in our present has a profound material, emotional, and spiritual impact on several generations down the lineage. This book integrates the ancient wisdom of the Hindu traditions with the latest insight psychology and psychoanalysis offer in understanding the dynamic of family karma and how to resolve it.

In our psychiatric and analytic practices, we have worked with many women and men who have carried the burden of their family's best achievements, worst failures, and unrealized dreams. They have · learned to identify all kinds of ancestral legacies that divert them from actualizing their unique mix of innate potentials. When these women and men recognized their karmic inheritance and settled their family's karmic accounts, they cleared the way to redirect their energies more in accord with their true path and passion, their soul's calling.

The first three chapters of this book provide a general introduction to the subject of family blessings and curses that we illustrate with case examples, including some of the our own experiences with our ancestral legacy. Chapter 4 deals with ancestral karma; in chapter 5, we discuss the family and seven kundalini chakras. In chapters 6, 7, and 8, we offer several approaches you can take to identify and then work with the karmic inheritance of your parents and grandparents.

To paraphrase Lord Krishna's advice to Arjuna, his protégé in the Bhagavad Gita (3:35): Your own soul path, even if you don't follow it perfectly, is better than someone else's soul path, even though you never miss a step.

Part One

TRACING YOUR FAMILY KARMA

I

BEGINNING THE WORK OF
RETIRING YOUR FAMILY KARMA

One of the major tenets of modern psychotherapy is that each of us is responsible for our behavior and destiny. All too often our patients tell us, "I did it to myself; I'm responsible." This is true for the consequences of our actions; but, as you will see in the following chapters, all of us inherit burdens and blessings that we did not create, not to mention that life, even under the best of conditions, is difficult.

Taking personal responsibility for our life coincides well with the Western ethos of individual freedom, initiative, accountability, and authority. This formula generally works well in dealing with the *conscious* aspects of our personality and relationships, and with the consequences of our actions. But how can a person choose, control, and regulate what is beyond individual consciousness? What happened before we were born? The effects of choices our ancestors made?

The dogged insistence on personal responsibility for choices and consequences is admirable; however, this insistence can also obstruct investigation and reflection upon causes beyond our personal choice. Although there are ways we can gain access to what is outside our immediate consciousness (that is, the "unconscious"), how are we to deal with issues that come from beyond our personal experience in this lifetime?

Each of us has the opportunity and the challenge of working on ourselves as well as our ancestors' unfinished tasks, all the while perpetuating their worthy achievements. We can either carry forward an evolutionary trajectory that improves life, or we can repeat family patterns that constrict us and coerce our descendants. Ideally, our goal as conscious adults is to resolve the problems with which our ancestors struggled—virulent complexes, relationship problems, chakra imbalances, medical and psychiatric conditions—*and* develop and express our innate potentials and gifts to the extent we are capable, given the circumstances into which we are born, grow up, and live our lives. Our task is to retain from the legacy of our family what furthers the expression of our innate talent and reject what thwarts progress on our soul's journey.

When we are not able to continue the family line in a personally authentic manner, the psyche and/or body can rebel in the form of medical and psychiatric problems, relationship difficulties, various sorts of under-performance or failure, and lowered physical and emotional vitality. However, when we choose the evolutionary path, we have the opportunity to retire the curse and the suffering of our ancestors, perpetuate their spiritual and creative legacy, and become our authentic selves: individuals who have realized as far as possible our innate predisposition and particular mix of talents and gifts.

To the extent we succeed in taking the evolutionary path, we rid collective consciousness and the unconscious of the cumulative psychic toxicity of our ancestors' problems, further their laudable accomplishments (their "good" karma), and leave the planet a more conscious, better informed, and safer place to live. In order to retire family karma, however, we have to be able to recognize its manifestations in our lives and find ways of retiring it.

In this book, we will first explore the concept of karma, how it generally works, and we'll provide examples from myth and real life that illustrate the effects of family karma. We will then explain the sources of family karma, how it manifests psychologically in our lives and its link to our physiological make-up through our chakras. Throughout, we provide stories from our clients who have worked through their family karma issues. It is our hope that their examples will help you identify your own family karma and take the necessary action to lift the curses and harvest the blessings you have inherited.

HOW TO USE THIS BOOK

As you read this book, you will find journal exercises to help you apply what you're learning to your own situation. Our clients' stories may give you some important insights into your life patterns and story. Therefore, we suggest that you get yourself a good-sized notebook and dedicate it to your family karma exploration.

Journal Exercise: Are You Locked into Your Family Karma?

In exploring your family karma, begin with yourself. At this point, we invite you to answer the following ten questions, each on a separate page in your journal, before you continue with the rest of the book. These questions point to some of the damaging effects of family patterns that can and do extend over more than two generations. Answer these questions now to the best of your ability. After you have read the rest of the book, we would like you to answer these ten questions again and compare your new answers with your first responses.

1. Describe your grandparents' relationship. What similarities and/or differences do you recognize between their relationship and your intimate relationship(s)?

2. How do/did each of your grandparents react emotionally to various situations? Do you find yourself reacting in similar ways, even though your reactions don't make any sense to you?

3. Recall and write down any dreams in which your father or mother, or grandfather or grandmother, does something noticeably out of character (i.e., differently than they act in waking life). This question will make more sense later when we discuss dreams and the information they can provide.

4. What physical ailments do you have that "run in the family" for which there appears to be no medical treatment?

5. What sort of work do you do? Who among your older relatives (parents, grandparents, aunts, and uncles) does/did the same sort of work you do? What do/did your older relatives say about the line of work you are in?

6. If you are an adopted child, what attitudes and behaviors do you have that have no precedent in your adoptive family?

7. What are the "ancestral dramas" in your family line? (For example, "Men in this family always/never..." "Our family does..." "The women in our family..." "Children are supposed to...")

8. How do you relate to, or what do you feel about, your family traditions? (For example, you like them; you rebel against them; they give you a sense of security; they stifle you; you believe you have to uphold them; etc.)

9. What functional as well as dysfunctional coping strategies do you share with other members of your (extended) family?

Functional coping strategies, for example, would be anticipating situations or consequences of actions; observing your emotions and behavior; being able to laugh rather than throw a tantrum. Dysfunctional coping strategies, for example, would be denial; blaming others; resorting to temper tantrums, excessive drinking, or gambling to manage stress.

10. If you have been in counseling or psychotherapy, what issues have you worked on? How effective has your counseling or psychotherapy been in resolving your issues of concern?

◆   ◆   ◆

In the following chapters, we provide you with tools for searching out the elements of your family blessings and curses—your clan karma—as well as numerous journal exercises to help you dig deeper into your family legacy and the effect it has had on you.

Welcome to the journey!

2

WHAT IS KARMA?

Erol is a proud, driven, successful man. He was raised in a lower middle-class family, and success was of primary importance to his parents and to him—more than anything else. Consequently, his work became increasingly important to him. Erol enjoyed the acclaim and power he gained on the job. As his son and his daughter entered their teen years, Erol found it more comfortable to retreat into his work than to deal with his energetic teenage children. Evelyn, Erol's wife, took on more and more responsibilities for rearing and disciplining the children as Erol spent ever-longer hours at work. Rumor had it that he might have been getting too close to one of the younger women work associates.

Evelyn pleaded repeatedly for Erol to take more interest in their children and in their marriage, but to no avail. The harder she tried, the more he thought of her as a nag, and retreated deeper into his financially rewarding work. His son, at age 14, started doing drugs. His daughter got pregnant when she was 16 and had an abortion. Evelyn became depressed and sought psychiatric treatment. Finally, she filed divorce papers, and asked Erol to move out. Two weeks later, Erol had a major heart attack.

While Erol was in cardiac rehab, his cardiologist insisted he see someone for psychotherapy. In his therapy, Erol explored the consequences of his choice to pursue professional growth at the expense of his personal life and relationships. He admitted there were many possibilities in life he had not taken time to cultivate. He recognized that his parents' distress at their very modest circumstances had contributed to the high value they placed on material success. He remembered how his father's sense of failure as a provider and his hopes that Erol would have a financially more rewarding life had driven him since he was in high school. As Erol learned more about his father's childhood and youth, he saw that his father's parents had worked hard but had always lived hand-to-mouth. His relentless success drive, he realized, was part of a family pattern extending back at least two generations.

Like many women of her generation, Evelyn came from a middle-class family where her father was the wage earner and mother, the homemaker. Evelyn's parents had met in college and married soon after graduation. Although Evelyn's mother had a fine college education, she worked only a couple of years after marriage. When her first child was born, she quit work. From then on, she devoted her energies to child rearing, homemaking, and, when her children got older, she volunteered her services in her church and community.

Evelyn did not want a life like the one her mother had. She recognized that her mother felt she had missed out on some areas of personal growth that a job outside the home, commensurate with her education, would have offered. Evelyn had often felt the sting of her mother's ambivalent comments about Evelyn's attempt to balance family and job. On the one hand, her mother was proud of Evelyn as a mother, wife, and working woman; but on the other, she criticized Evelyn for not being involved in church and community work as she had been, and hinted that some of the distress in Evelyn's marriage was the consequence of not being the kind of wife that Erol needed and deserved. About a year before she filed the divorce papers, Evelyn had entered psychotherapy to deal with her increasing depression.

After several months' hard work in individual psychotherapy, Erol asked Evelyn if she would be willing to go with him to a marriage counselor. He told her he had learned a lot about himself. He wanted to work with her on rebuilding their marriage.

In our clinical practice, we have seen many women and men like Evelyn and Erol who feel they have to make choices that lead to results they hadn't intended. As they discover more about their attitudes and values, they often identify family habits and patterns that had influenced them much more than they had realized.

Of course, your ancestors can and do leave behavioral and attitudinal legacies that help you actualize your innate potentials. But it is in the nature of our work as psychotherapists and psychoanalysts that, initially at least, our clients seek help with their immediate problems and struggles. As part of our work with our clients, however, we attempt to help them gain a differentiated view of their parents, grandparents, and other forebears. Mingled with ancestral legacies we discover blessings as well as curses. You can take a major step toward maturing when you can see and accept both the good and the bad in other important people in your life and lineage.

Life is a series of choices. Choices lead to actions. Actions carry consequences. Action plus consequence is what we call *karma*. The results of many of our actions affect not only us, but others as well. The consequences of many of our grandparents' and our parents' actions reverberate in our lives today. In this book we will use the term "karma" to refer to our ancestors' and our own actions and the consequences that necessarily follow. A lot of karma spans three or more generations. That is why we call it "family karma."

MEANS AND ENDS

When you choose a course of action, you have in mind some desired end or goal. You base your action on the information you perceive to be relevant to your chosen goal. Your goal appears to be some improvement, some enhancement in your life, some valued outcome. Whether or not your actions attain the desired results may be another question. Like wonder drugs that combat a specific illness but can have undesirable side effects, your actions can also have unintended consequences. Be that as it may, karma—choice, action, and consequence—is embedded in an interactive matrix of perceptions and values. Moreover, every sequence of perception and value-based, goal-oriented action creates an outcome that is itself a situation, resembling or differing from the earlier situation in which you took action. Thus, you can see how your life is an unending cycle of actions and outcomes, all based on what you value and what you perceive.

At one level, nobody questions this truth: If you kick a dog, it will yelp. If you treat people badly, you can expect them to respond in kind. But karma operates at many levels, and the consequences do not always immediately follow your actions. Karma can pass down through a family from generation to generation. That is to say, one generation after another may repeat a pattern of actions and suffer or enjoy the inevitable consequences that follow those actions. Indeed, we are responsible for much of our karma, but we can also inherit karma from our ancestors or from a past life.

THE THREE SOURCES OF KARMA

In our clinical experience working with hundreds of patients, we have found three sources of karma that each of us must address in order to reach our fullest and highest soul potential: individual, family, and past-life karma.

First, you must retire the karma you have generated in your present life. This is your personal karma. As you recognize conditions and situations you have created that are uncomfortable, that do not serve you well, that cause you distress, you must take the steps necessary to change those conditions and situations. Perhaps you find yourself in a line of work that does not really suit you. Maybe you have become obsessed in an activity, a cause, a relationship. You may have hurt others and only you can alleviate that pain through sincere words and actions. Whatever it is, wherever you see the undesirable fruits of your actions, it is up to you to retire your karma by taking remedial actions that will lead to more desirable outcomes.

Second, you have to work on the karma of your family—parents, grandparents, and other forebears—to free your soul from their unintended karma. Perhaps you are fulfilling the ambition of a grandparent rather than your own. It sometimes happens that you deal with situations in "family-typical" ways that you later recognize do not suit you, that may even be contrary to what you deep-down feel is authentically your way. Or you might engage in behaviors that you consciously recognize as self-defeating but that you feel powerless to overcome. Many of our patients have experienced great relief when they have been able to trace such patterns in their lives to their ancestors who had similar patterns, attitudes, complexes, illnesses, relationship styles, and so forth. But you cannot change what you haven't identified. Recognizing the blessings and curses of your ancestors—your family karma—is the first step and often a revelation.

Third, you have to retire the karma generated in previous lives, your past-life karma. In the last few years, researchers have compiled persuasive evidence that supports the idea of past lives and karma deriving from them. For some people, past lives are an article of belief; for other people, the idea of past lives is nonsense. But if the empirical evidence so far accumulated continues to be supported by future research, more people will have to take the possibility of past life karma seriously.

When you realize that your life is encumbered by the results of your and other peoples' choices, or the residue from a past life, you can begin to make different choices that heal wounds, right wrongs, and— we hope—lead you to experience a fuller reality in which you live with greater integrity and authenticity.

Individual Karma

Jim is a recently retired businessman who had just sold his very successful company. He had amassed a large sum of money, and had hoped to enjoy life with his wife, children, grandchildren, and friends. In his heyday, he had been a ruthless entrepreneur who was focused on his work at the expense of all other aspects of his life. His wife—though loving and committed—had found other interests and friendships to fill the void that Jim's absence had created. His children had married and moved to the opposite coasts of the U.S. Jim really had no friends. At age 59, with his stash of money, good health, and a long life expectancy, Jim was the most lonely man on this planet. He was all dressed up with nowhere to go. At this point, he called to make an appointment for psychotherapy. He was caught in his own karmic trap.

We make choices in the pursuit of wealth, relationships, power, success, or other goals that often result in our neglecting some other possibilities and innate potentials that do not fit neatly in our chosen success program. Both what we have devoted our energies to and what we have neglected generate our individual karma. In realizing that what we attain often amounts to less than we had envisioned, we can harvest important insights. It is often in the margins of life that we discover the path to the center. We find the gold in the garbage.

Individual karma is our responsibility: we set it in motion; we pay the price. For example, consider the person who has no friends. This person might bewail his or her fate; might blame others; might become cynical, bitter, and morose. But what does it take to make friends? Friendship develops as we cultivate it with someone through openness, concern, shared interests, honesty, and enjoyment of each other. To cultivate a friendship, we must take the initiative part of the time. We must listen to our friend, as well as need our friend to listen to us. Friendship is a two-way street. The person who has no friends has not, for whatever reason, developed the necessary skills of mutuality. The consequence is lack of friends. Have we not heard people say of a lonely, grumpy person, "He brought it on himself"?

Family Karma

It may seem weird that we bear the consequences of what our ancestors did. Obviously, if they immigrated to the U.S., we were not born in the country of their birth. If they made it big and set up a trust fund for us, we benefit from it now. But our ancestors made other choices and took other actions that established patterns or energy fields that may continue to affect our thoughts, emotions, choices, and behaviors.

The idea underlying the concept of family karma is that the choices we make affect our children and possibly our grandchildren as well as us. Vice-versa, our parents', grandparents', and sometimes other ancestors' choices likewise carry consequences with which we still have to deal—as curses or blessings. We are the bearers of an ancestral karma that we must manage, either by retiring the curse or by enhancing the blessing. Each generation must carry forward the evolutionary trajectory of the family line, making the best use of the ancestral blessings and dissolving the ancestral curses. As long as we are unaware of ancestral patterns, we cannot modify their influence on us. In other words, we are unconscious of a lot family karma. To put it more precisely: much family karma operates outside our awareness from the psychic unknown, unconsciously.

We devote the body of this book to exploring the several ways in which we inherit family karma. For starters, however, we want to tell you of one of the most surprising and convincing testimonies for the reality of family karma that we discovered: the family karma of adopted children.

The Karma of Adopted Children

Mutual friends of ours have an adopted daughter who experienced difficulties as a teenager and young adult. Our friends wracked their brains trying to understand why their adopted child was dealing with her difficulties in such self-destructive ways. "What did we do wrong?" they asked themselves, typically trying to take responsibility.

Yet, regardless how often they searched their souls, they could find no satisfactory explanation for their daughter's destructive attempts to manage her distress. In the course of their suffering, the adopted daughter located her birth parents. To everybody's surprise, her birth mother had resorted to the same dysfunctional coping strategies by abusing drugs when her life problems threatened to overwhelm her. Although the daughter had been adopted shortly after birth, and consequently had not learned these coping mechanisms from her birth mother, under stress she resorted to the same means that her mother had chosen! Since this was not a learned behavior, the only satisfactory explanation was family karma.

Past Life Karma

For the Western reader, past lives may be a very speculative hypothesis. However, we have found in working with individual patients that even after their individual and family karma is retired, often there persists a residue of karma we cannot explain on the basis of these two frameworks. Such karma may be the residue from a past life.

Boris Matthews' Testimony to Past-Life Experience

Up until young adulthood, I had a persistent fantasy that I finally began to understand as possibly deriving from a past life. The fantasy was that if people knew what I was feeling and thinking, they would pry paving stones up from the street and hurl them at me. I had never lived where there were cobblestone streets, nor had other children ever thrown stones at me. It took me a long time to begin to question the absoluteness of the fantasy. Only when I experimented by telling "safe" people some of my fears of being stoned on the street did I begin to discover that they did not "throw stones" at me. Gradually, I began to see that what I had taken for a certainty was in fact a belief the origin of which I could not pinpoint, except to hypothesize that it might have come from an actual experience in some past life.

Many years have now passed since I last experienced that fantasy. Since then, I have come to feel much more safe and secure in the world as I have let other people into my "interior" world and discovered that most of them have no intention of hurting me. In fact, some of them even like me!

Professor Ian Stevenson has conducted meticulous studies of more than 3,000 cases of possible reincarnation, reporting only those that meet his high research standards.[1] For example, children between the ages of 2 and 5 years sometimes exhibit phobias that do not derive from imitating another member of the family or from any postnatal traumatic experiences. "The phobias nearly always corresponded to the mode of death in the life of the deceased person the child claimed to remember."[2] Play that is unusual for the child's family, for which the child had no model, also sometimes can be traced to a past life. "The play accorded with claimed memories of previous lives expressed by the children when they could speak. . . . In 22 cases [of 66 cases of unusual play] the child's statement were found to match events in the life of a specific deceased person. In such cases the play was found to correspond to some aspects of that deceased person's life, such as his or her vocation, avocation, or mode of death."[3]

Birthmarks and birth defects sometimes correspond to wounds on deceased persons. "About 35% of children who claim to remember previous lives have birthmarks and/or birth defects that they . . . attribute to wounds on a person whose life the child remembers."[4] Of 49 cases in which a medical report on the deceased person was available, 43 showed correspondences between birthmarks and/or birth defects and the wounds of the deceased.[5] In a study from India, the correspondences between birthmarks or birth defects corresponded to the matching wounds on the deceased person. "Two subjects had major birth defects. One was born without his right hand and right forearm; another had a severe malformation of the spine (kyphosis) and prominent birthmark on the head. The remaining eight subjects had birthmarks corresponding to gunshot wounds, knife wounds, burns, and injuries in a vehicular accident. . . . The hypothesis of reincarnation seems best to explain all features of cases."[6]

As researchers and clinicians investigate this fascinating subject further, we may get better guidelines for understanding and managing past life karma. But for now, we hold this out as a hypothesis and a hope for deeper understanding of human suffering and the evolution of the soul. Regardless where our karma comes—personal, family, or past life—we have to retire it, now or later.

Karma—whether personal, family, or past life—functions in a context or matrix that we need to understand to get a fuller sense of how karma works.

THE MATRIX OF KARMA

To get what we want, we have to do what is necessary. To avoid what we don't want, we must act in ways that do not take us where we do not want to end up. Whatever we do, sooner or later we begin to sense that what we have striven for is not the be-all and end-all that we had imagined. We begin to ask whether there is more to life than what we envisioned. The reality we have experienced appears to offer less than what it seemed to promise. There are three components of the karmic matrix:

1. We act in the belief that our choices will lead to a fuller, richer life;

2. The reality we perceive and act on is limited;

3. Our actions sometimes lead to desirable, and sometimes to undesirable, outcomes.

We have already discussed the third point—karma. To appreciate the karmic matrix, we must understand the first and second elements: the notion of a richer, fuller life, and the idea of perceiving a limited reality.

Limited Reality: Maya

With the insight that our reality is limited or partial, we begin to suspect that what we have believed is the whole of reality may not be the whole of reality. This is what *maya* means: our space-time world is indeed solid and something we have to come to terms with, but it is not the whole of reality. It is a limited reality. Perhaps we now recognize that we have lost ourselves—or important parts of ourselves—in our pursuit (or avoidance) of the rewards with which our space-time world tempts us. Now we see there are other choices we could make, such as attempting to discover and then follow our own soul path: our *dharma*.

The Vision of a Fuller Life: Dharma

The goal of life is to move from preoccupation with a limited reality to participation in the richness of being: realization of our individual potential; living each stage of life to its fullest; participation in our community; and attainment of spiritual maturity. The term dharma embraces these four dimensions: individual, developmental, community, and spiritual. It is our dharma to actualize our innate potential, to become the unique individual we potentially are, to realize and live our various talents and gifts, neither pushing ourselves beyond our limits nor living beneath our capacities. It is our dharma to "act our age," to be teenagers when we are teenagers (not when we are 45), to be youthful when young, wise when old. It is our dharma to find our place in our community as interdependent creatures. And it is our dharma to recognize that we participate in the greater scheme of Being Whose spiritual laws govern all creation.[7]

In the course of life, we are continually cycling through the karmic matrix. We act on the basis of what we value and perceive, attempting to further attain what we value. Our actions bear fruits that we evaluate. Our evaluations may alter what we perceive as reality, which now becomes the basis for new perceptions and actions and outcomes. Again and again we retrace the cycle of maya (our limited view of reality), karma (our actions and the outcomes), and dharma (the drive for fulfillment) in all its dimensions.

Take some time now, before you read farther, to work in your journal and think about your life: the choices you have made, the actions you have taken, what they have gotten you, and the purpose of it all.

INTRODUCTION TO THE JOURNAL EXERCISES

Throughout this book, you will find journal exercises. We have included them as a means for you to explore the topics we discuss in the various chapters. The value of keeping a journal is that you have a record of your discoveries, and you can monitor and chart the changes you experience.

Journal Exercise: Looking at Your Values and Your Reality

Our vision of reality is always limited. But we have to make choices and take actions at any give time on the basis of our notion of reality. This exercise will help you see more clearly how your vision of a fuller life—your values, in short—have influenced your perception of reality and your choices and actions.

Now open your journal so that you have both left- and right-facing blank pages. Divide each page down the middle so that you have two columns on each page. On the left-hand page, title the first column "My Reality." Title the second column on the left-hand page "Choices and Actions That Created My Reality." On the right-hand page, title the first column "How Well My Reality Suits Me Now," and title the last column "Different Actions for Different Consequences."

We will take Erol's situation, which we discussed earlier, and briefly work out this exercise as an example of how it might look.

Erol's Reality and Values

My Reality

Have good financial security. • Not much relationship with my wife or children. • Son started taking drugs. • Daughter got pregnant. • Had a heart attack.

Choices & Actions That Created My Reality

Worked hard to not end up like my folks. Didn't think spending time with the kids or wife was too important. Believed that a solid financial base would make for a satisfying life free from worry. My son said he was trying to get my attention. Didn't take care of my health; worked all the time.

How Well My Reality Suits Me Now

Kids and wife are pissed, and I've had a heart attack. This isn't the way it's supposed to be.

Different Actions for Different Consequences

Working in therapy and couples counseling; taking better care of my health. Maybe financial success isn't everything. Had an outing with my son, and it wasn't too bad.

There are four broad areas of your "Reality" you can address in this exercise. One area is your innate potential: your talents, interests, skills. A second area is your stage in life. Your participation in your various communities is the third area. Lastly, your understanding of spirituality determines the values that condition your perception of what is real and hence the choices you make and the actions you take.

We deal with cycles of maya, karma, and dharma as we learn from and retire the consequences of bad choices, or reap the harvest of good choices, and more fully satisfy the various aspects of our soul's calling, our dharma. In the course of these never-ending cycles, we may notice that we repeat or reverse old patterns.

REPETITION AND REVERSAL

The example of our friends' adopted daughter reveals one of the faces of family karma: repetition. The daughter repeated her birth parent's behaviors, but not through modeling on parental example. (In chapter 4, we will discuss one possible way in which this repetition might operate.) Family karma shows us another face, however: a reversal, or turn to an opposite behavior. Earlier, we alluded to children of unsuccessful parents who achieve much in their lives.

Family karma is like a sacred (or demonic) serpent chasing its own tail: repetition and reversal, an endless cycle of virtuosity and villainy. We may get stuck repeating our ancestors' lives, and/or we feel compelled to live "opposite" kinds of lives from what they led. These processes can operate either consciously or unconsciously. In other words, parents may consciously want their children (us!) to pursue their dreams, legacies, and expectations; or they may unconsciously will their children (us!) to live out their unlived life potentials.

For their part, the children may consciously live out or rebel against parental expectations, or be unconsciously entangled in the web of unconscious parental issues. Conscious and unconscious repetition and reversal create an intricate, interacting web among ancestors and their offspring. Often it takes half a lifetime to disentangle ourselves and clearly recognize our own path and destiny. But don't be discouraged: you can do it with awareness, knowledge and responsibility.

3

EVIDENCE FOR FAMILY KARMA
IN ANCIENT AND MODERN LEGENDS

There is an old saying that as the twig is bent, so the tree is inclined; that the apple does not fall far from the tree. Family karma refers to the same phenomenon as do these traditional sayings: our ancestors influence us in profound ways that can facilitate our realizing our innate gifts and talents, and thus actualize our potential; or their legacy can burden us in ways that hinder the development and manifestation of our authentic nature.

Family karma is the family legacy, tradition, blessing or curse that binds its members, often unconsciously, but nevertheless relentlessly. Family karma fuels the feud between the Montagues and the Capulets in Shakespeare's *Romeo and Juliet*. Family karma is the vendetta between the Hattfields and the McCoys. In Greek mythology, we see family karma most vividly in the story of the House of Atreus. We also find several stories of family karma in the Bible.

FAMILY KARMA IN THE BIBLE

Psalm 79 is a "national lament" that is a clear example of family karma. The pagans have laid waste to Jerusalem and desecrated its temple. The Psalmist implores Yahweh to put an end to his people's sufferings, to "pour out your anger on the pagans, who do not acknowledge you." "*Do not,*" the Psalmist pleads, "*hold our ancestors' crimes against us.*"[1] In other words, exempt us from our family karma. In Isaiah, Yahweh promises not to "be silent until I have settled my account with them for their sins and their fathers' sins . . . those men who burned incense on the mountains and insulted me on the hills. I will pay them back in full all they deserve."[2]

The Book of Daniel tells the story of a young Hebrew captured by the Babylonian King Nebuchadnezzar. Daniel and three other young men found favor with the King, and became members of the King's court, where Daniel interpreted visions and dreams for Nebuchadnezzar. In Chapter 9, Daniel ponders the fate of the Hebrews, the destruction of Jerusalem, and the fact that "the whole of Israel has flouted Your Law and turned away, unwilling to listen to Your voice." Daniel confesses his and his peoples' sins (the sins of the ancestors), ardently praying to Yahweh to forgive his people. Daniel endures many visions and trials, including being cast into the lion pit. Yet, after six days, he is still unharmed. Seeing this, the King exclaims, "O Lord, God of Daniel, there is no god but you!"[3] And Daniel survived the ordeals of a hero.

FAMILY KARMA IN THE HOUSE OF ATREUS

Another powerful, enduring, and well-known account of family karma in Greek mythology is the saga of ill-fated House of Atreus. The cause of its bloody misfortunes was said to be a horrible deed committed by Tantalus, King of Lydia. The evil that Tantalus had committed plagued his descendents for many generations. It was as though a curse hung over the House of Atreus so that his children and children's children likewise committed evil in spite of themselves.

Tantalus, the son of Zeus, was honored by the gods. They even let him dine at their table on Olympus, tasting the ambrosia and nectar otherwise reserved exclusively for the gods. Once, Tantalus invited the gods to dine at his table. In return for their favor, Tantalus committed an outrage, perhaps driven by some passion of hatred or envy of them.

Tantalus had only one son, Pelops. He had Pelops slain, boiled, and served to the gods at his table. Perhaps he wanted to show them how easy it would be to deceive them; but whatever his motivation, Tantalus never dreamed that his guests would recognize the food he had set before them.

But the gods knew. They drew back from the ghastly banquet and turned upon Tantalus, declaring that he should be so punished that no man after him would ever dare commit such an outrage: the gods condemned Tantalus to a pool in Hades over which hung lush fruit. But whenever Tantalus reached for the fruit, it receded from his grasp, and if he bent down to drink, the waters of the pool drained away. Thus he stood forever, tormented by undying thirst and hunger, food and drink always just beyond his reach (hence the word, "tantalize.")

The gods restored Pelops to life, and the remainder of his days were successful. He was the only one of Tantalus' descendants not marked by misfortune. Pelops had two sons, Atreus and Thyestes. The evil inheritance of their grandfather descended on them in full force. (To follow the complicated story, it will help to refer to the annotated family tree in figure 1, page 24.)

Atreus was king; Thyestes, his brother, had no power. For whatever reason, Thyestes fell in love with Atreus's wife and successfully wooed her. Atreus found out and swore that his brother should pay as no man ever had: he killed his brother's two little children, had them cut from limb to limb, boiled, and served to their father. Here we see the repetition of Tantalus's murder of Pelops. When Thyestes learned what he had eaten, he vomited the flesh, cried out, and called down a curse upon the house of his brother, Atreus. During Atreus's lifetime the horrible deed was not avenged, but Atreus' children and grandchildren suffered. As we will see later in several case examples, the consequences of an act do not always befall the perpetrator, but his or her children or grandchildren.

Atreus had two sons, Menelaus and Agamemnon. Menelaus married Helen after the Trojan War and took her back to Sparta where they

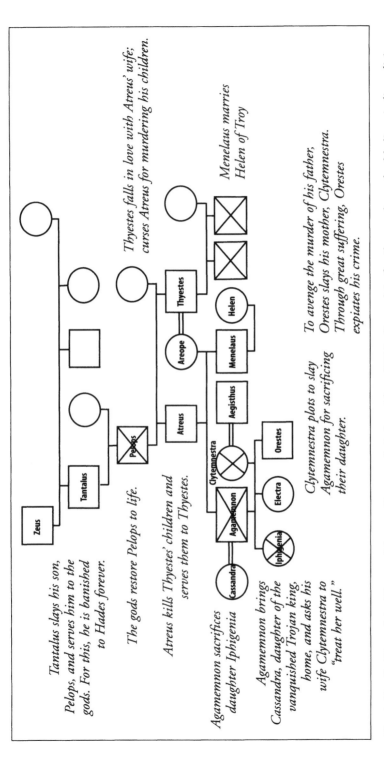

Fig. 1. Family Tree of the House of Atreus. Boxes and circles with an "X" indicate slain family members; double lines indicate liaisons.

lived ever after. Agamemnon's fate was far different. There are two accounts of Agamemnon's death. The sordid, older tale tells of Agamemnon dying at the hands of his wife's lover. But the classical account, *The Oresteia*, written by Aeschylus about 450 B.C., is the one most familiar and revealing of family karma, for Agamemnon had stained his hands with blood some ten years before his inglorious death.

The great city of Troy lay in what is now modern Turkey, at the eastern end of the Mediterranean. The fabled ten-year war between the Greeks and the Trojans came about, as do so many Greek tragedies, when Eris, goddess of Discord (who was not popular among the other Olympian gods) was offended by being excluded from a marriage banquet. "Beware the gods not honored" is ancient and sage advice. Eris threw a golden apple into the wedding assembly. Upon it was written, "For the Fairest."

Of course, all the goddesses wanted it, but the contest came down to three: Hera, Aphrodite, and Pallas Athena. Zeus knew he would surely offend two if he were to choose one from among them, and so he directed them to go to Mount Ida, near Troy, where a young prince, Paris, was tending his father's sheep. Paris would have to make the fateful choice. Being young, he responded as young men often do: not to the wisdom and fighting spirit of Pallas Athena, who offered to lead the Trojans to victory over the Greeks; nor to Hera, patron of conjugal fidelity and family, who promised him lordship over Europe and Asia; but to Aphrodite, goddess of beauty and pleasure, who promised him the fairest woman in the world—Helen, Menelaus' wife. To her Paris handed the golden apple.

Now, Helen was the wife of Menelaus, son of Atreus and brother of Agamemnon. Aphrodite led unsuspecting Paris to Sparta, where Menelaus and Helen received him as a guest. Trusting Paris's honor and the ties between guest and host, Menelaus went off to Crete, but when he returned home, he discovered Helen had been abducted by Paris. Menelaus summoned all the chieftains of Greece to honor their vows and join him in laying waste to the Trojans.

The chieftains assembled, some reluctant to go to war over the abduction of a woman, but they eventually rallied around the cause. They readied a great fleet to carry them across the sea to the shores of Troy. Yet day after day a fierce north wind blew, and the dangerous tides held the Greek armada hostage. Finally Calchas, a soothsayer, declared the gods had spoken to him. The sacrifice of a royal maiden was necessary to appease the goddess Artemis, and the royal maiden was to be Iphigenia, daughter of Agamemnon, leader of the Greek army.

Agamemnon anguished. To slay his own daughter, stain his hands with the blood of his own child, horrified him. Yet Agamemnon's reputation with his army was at stake; Agamemnon's ambition to conquer Troy was great. And so the father sent for his daughter, telling her that he had arranged a great marriage for her, to Achilles, the best and greatest of all the Greek chieftains. Again, we see a parent using his child for his own ends, just as Atreus and Tantalus had done.

But when Iphigenia arrived, the altar was for sacrifice and not marriage. Iphigenia died, the winds quieted, the seas calmed, and the Greek ships sailed for Troy.

The Greeks and the Trojans battled for ten years. The gods took sides. Earth and Olympus were in turmoil. Sometimes the Greeks appeared to gain; other times the Trojans seemed to be winning. Ultimately, however, the Greeks vanquished the Trojan forces, sacked the city, and returned home to Greece, where the curse of the House of Atreus claimed more victims.

Angered at the murder of her daughter, Agamemnon's wife, Clytemnestra, had taken a lover in his absence. According to *The Oresteia*, upon Agamemnon's arrival home, Clytemnestra deceitfully welcomed her long-absent husband, who had brought with him a prize, a gift from his army: Cassandra, daughter of the vanquished Trojan king, Priam. "Treat her well," Agamemnon told his wife and entered his house. Then, from within the house the cry of a man in agony rang out, followed by silence. The door opened, Clytemnestra appeared, blood smeared on her hands, face, dress. Clytemnestra had taken revenge on Agamemnon for the death of Iphigenia, her daughter.

Clytemnestra and Agamemnon had two other children besides Iphigenia—another daughter, Electra, and a son, Orestes. Orestes had been sent away; Electra had remained, but suffered a miserable existence with her mother and her mother's lover. Her hope had rested on Orestes: when would he return and bring justice?

As Orestes grew, he felt ever more painfully the injustice. Orestes stood between two horrible choices. It was a son's duty to avenge his father's murder; yet that meant slaying his mother, an act abhorrent to humans and gods alike. In his agony, Orestes journeyed to Delphi to ask the oracle of Apollo to speak to him. The oracle was clear in its directive: Slay those who slew. Orestes knew what he had to do.

In disguise, Orestes and a friend returned to his father's house. Their plan was to deceive Clytemnestra by reporting that Orestes had died. That would gain them entrance to the house and the opportunity to draw their swords against Clytemnestra and her lover. The ruse worked. Orestes plunged his sword into his mother's breast, his friend slew her lover. But the horrible deed drove Orestes mad. He wandered many years, seeing before him snakes with eyes that dripped blood, which he believed his mother had sent to torture him.

After Orestes had wandered long and far, Apollo, who had commanded him to avenge the murder of his father, finally sent Orestes to Athens to plead his case before Athena, the patron of that city. His long suffering had purified his heart. As Orestes stood before Athena, Apollo stood beside him. "It was I," Apollo said, "who am answerable for what he did." Orestes listened calmly, but said, "I, not Apollo, was guilty of my mother's murder, but I have been cleansed of my guilt." Orestes had atoned through his suffering and by taking responsibility for his act. He went forth a free man. The curse of the House of Atreus was ended.

◆   ◆   ◆

In the myth of the House of Atreus we see the consequences of an ancestor's deeds passing from generation to generation until, finally, one member of the family lifts the karmic curse through his actions and his suffering. Perhaps the best-known "real-life" example of a family beset by the karma of an ancestor is the dynasty founded by Joseph P. Kennedy, Sr., father of John F. Kennedy, Robert F. Kennedy, and Edward M. Kennedy. The Kennedy story is in many ways a sequel to the myth of the House of Atreus.

VIOLENT DEATH IN THE KENNEDY DYNASTY

Many members of the Kennedy family—both in President Kennedy's and in the following generation—have come close to violent death or actually died violently. Generations of ruthless competition, deceit, using wealth to manipulate others, and womanizing contrasted with honorable and valuable public service. This created a karmic matrix in which ambitious Kennedys were willing to pay any price for success. Students of the Kennedy dynasty generally agree that this family pattern derives from Joseph P. Kennedy, Sr., his wife, Rose, and their parents. The cumulative consequences of their actions were violent death for some of them.

Joe Kennedy's eldest son, Joseph, Jr., died in 1944 while flying a test plane designed to be loaded with high explosives and directed to its target by remote control after the pilot and co-pilot bailed out. In the test plane, the electronic remote control detonation device was faulty. Although Joe, Jr., had been warned of the danger, he insisted on flying it. The plane exploded over England, killing Joe, Jr. and his co-pilot. To some people, it looked like suicide.[4]

In May, 1948, Joe Sr.'s daughter Kathleen and her friend Peter Fitzwilliam were flying from Le Bourget Airport in France to Paris to meet her father. Because a thunderstorm was predicted, commercial flights had been cancelled, but Fitzwilliam insisted on flying on to Paris anyway. Their plane went down in the Cévennes mountains in the storm. All were killed.[5]

On November 22, 1963, President John F. Kennedy was assassinated in Dallas, Texas. The country and the world mourned. The charming, young, bright, witty president had inspired a generation with his call to do for their country. In his brief tenure in office,

Kennedy negotiated a limited arms control agreement with the Soviet Union, revitalized relationships with Latin America, supported desegregation efforts, made the White House a center for the arts in America, and established the Peace Corps, to name only a few of his accomplishments.

Seymour Hersch writes, "Jack Kennedy was a dazzling figure as an adult, with stunning good looks, an inquisitive mind, and a biting sense of humor that was often self-mocking. He throve on adoration and surrounded himself with starstruck friends and collegues."[6] Yet, as we have found out in the years following his death, there was a dark side to JFK.[7] Jack Kennedy was a womanizer, like his father. He concealed his health problems and use of mood-altering drugs. His handling of the Cuban Missile Crisis—supposedly his "greatest triumph as president"—brought the U.S. and the Soviet Union to the brink of thermonuclear war that was avoided only when Premier Nikita Krushchev backed down.[8] John F. Kennedy paid dearly for his father's unbridled ambition.

Robert F. Kennedy, attorney general in JFK's administration, was shot in Los Angeles in 1968 while campaigning for the Democratic nomination for president. Under his leadership, he made fighting organized crime a high priority of the Department of Justice. In *The Enemy Within,* he wrote, "The paramount interest in self, in material wealth, in security must be replaced by an actual, not just a vocal, interest in our country, . . . by a will to fight what is evil, and a desire to serve."[9] Yet Robert F. Kennedy was the son and grandson of men who had been involved with organized crime for decades, and himself had contacts with organized crime.

Like his father and his brother, Robert Kennedy concealed whatever would harm the family image and myth. When President Kennedy was shot in Dallas, Robert was in Washington. He began "immediately to hide all evidence of Kennedy's secret life from the nation—as well as from the new president, who would be sitting in the Oval Office by early evening" of the assassination day.[10]

In June, 1964, Senator Edward (Ted) Kennedy—the youngest son of Joseph P. Kennedy, Sr.—insisted on flying in severe fog to Springfield, Massachusetts, to a Democratic convention. When the pilot refused, Senator Kennedy chartered a plane that crashed on the way to Springfield, killing the pilot and one of the Senator's aide's, as well as injuring Ted Kennedy and Senator of Indiana Birch Bayh and his wife. Senator Kennedy's womanizing is no secret, yet he is the "most remarkable" of Joseph P. Kennedy's sons: "The conscience of the Congress, [Senator Edward Kennedy] is the man who has steadily and with great conviction labored to achieve programs of social justice and equity that his father would have considered deeply suspect. Senator Kennedy has become an indispensable defender of American liberalism."[11]

In July, 1969, Senator Ted Kennedy effectively ended the family's hopes for another U.S. President from his generation of Kennedys when Mary Jo Kopechne died in a car Ted Kennedy was driving on Chappaquiddick Island. One of Robert's sons crashed into a tree while playing touch football on a ski slope in Colorado. In 1999, JFK's son, John, Jr., died in a plane crash while flying in bad weather from New York to Cape Cod.

In its obituary, the *Boston Herald* paid homage to Joseph P. Kennedy, Sr. as a man who, "in his own right and on his own terms, . . . rose from modest beginnings to the pinnacles of financial power and political eminence by adhering to old-fashioned American virtues that have been somewhat discounted in today's society: devotion to family, loyalty to friends, strength of character, and the will to win."[12] But Joe Kennedy's devotion to family was intended to serve his own ends; his loyalty to friends consisted in using people till he no longer needed them; the strength of his character lay in craftily pursuing his own ends.

The life of Joseph P. Kennedy, Sr. gives us some insight into the Kennedy karma. In the funeral oration for Caesar, Shakespeare gives Anthony lines that aptly express much of the essence of Joe Kennedy:

But 'tis a common proof
That lowliness is young ambition's ladder,
Whereto the climber-upward turns his face;
But when he once attains the upmost round
He then unto the ladder turns his back,
Looks in the clouds, scorning the base degrees
By which he did ascend. [13]

Although his personal origins were not lowly—his father was a prosperous Boston Irishman who had made his money in liquor and had achieved political office—Joe Kennedy always portrayed himself as a Horatio Alger who had risen from meager beginnings to wealth and influence. Kennedy never achieved the power of a Caesar, yet he ardently desired it; but "because of his character flaws, [he could] grasp it only through his sons as surrogates."[14]

Throughout his life, Joe Kennedy amassed wealth, bought, deceived, flattered, cultivated—and used—people who could advance his aims, while relentlessly grooming his sons for positions of political power.[15] Ronald Kessler writes, "Joe Kennedy orchestrated his sons' destinies. It was his edict that they rise, like salmon swimming upstream, to the top of American government. As a silent partner, Joe Kennedy provided all the cash and connections they needed to take advantage of their natural gifts, and he financed and directed their campaigns."[16] Of Jack Kennedy's election as president, his father, Joe, said, "I got Jack into politics. I was the one. . . . I told him Joe Jr. was deceased and that it was therefore his responsibility to run for Congress. He didn't want to. He felt he didn't have the ability, and he still feels that way. But I told him he had to."[17] And after he was elected, Jack Kennedy was undecided as to how to reward his brother, Robert, for his unstinting support and work in the election campaign. Joe overheard Jack ruminating to a friend. Joe called Jack to him and said, "I want to tell you, your brother Bobby busted his ass for you. He gave you his life blood. You know it, and I know it. By God, he deserves to be attorney general of the U.S., and by God, that's what he's going to be. Do you understand that?" And Jack said, "Yes, sir."[18]

There was never any question about Joseph P. Kennedy's will to win. "For Joe, it was not how you play the game but whether you win or lose."[19] Winning at all costs was a trait throughout his life that he instilled in his children, at a terribly high cost.

In the Bible accounts, the Greek myth of the House of Atreus, and the Kennedy family story, we have seen how "the sins" of the ancestors are visited upon the children. Family karma is an age-old phenomenon. In the next two chapters, we'll look for answers to the question: "How is family karma passed on to the descendants?"

4

EXPLORING THE FAMILY DYNAMICS
AND OUR RELATIONSHIPS

When we begin to suspect that the choices we have made were not fully our choices we may even say, "I felt I had to!" "I didn't have a choice!" As we reflect on the life we have lived, we start to recognize that we grew up in a certain climate of tacit or explicit expectations; of ways of doing things; of family myths and prejudices. We begin to recognize our family's emotional or medical or occupational patterns that extend over two or more generations. These insights prompt us to explore the karma of our family, the legacy that our grandparents and parents have left for us, their children.

So far, we have discussed the curse and the burden of family karma. But this is only one side of the coin. The other side is the blessing and the benefit of our ancestral karma. While the burden of family karma restricts us from attending to certain aspects of our potential, this in itself helps us focus on the karma at hand. In a sense, we become specialists! Our family karma restricts our field of psychological vision and area of enterprise. But in doing so, it forces us to attend to and circle around its subject matter. This restriction and focused amplification creates a high energy system for us around our family karma. The crucial task, however, is for us to maintain the tension between the calling to our individuation and the burden of our family karma. When we hold the tension of these opposing forces in our life, something very important emerges that transforms and transcends them both: our unique calling. So, as individuals, we face the twofold task of retiring the burdensome karma of our parents and other ancestors while discovering our soul's calling. This twofold task is indeed a work in progress, the opus of individuation, of actualizing our in-born potentials.

THE AUTHORS' EXPERIENCE WITH FAMILY KARMA

Our interest in family karma is more than professional. Each of us, in our own ways, has had to face the reality of the karmic blessings and burdens we inherited from our ancestors. Recognizing the karmic inheritance of our family—both the excessive blessings and the shackling curses—continues to demand our courage and our best efforts. Although we are psychotherapists, we are not different from you; all of us face the same challenges, although they differ in content and detail.

Ashok Bedi: My Story of Family Karma

The first phase of my life was burdened by attempts to deal with my father's and my mother's unresolved karmic issues. My father struggled with problems of survival, security, autonomy, and enterprise. Interestingly, my father ran a marginally successful restaurant business. However, this did permit him to serve to the poor who were the regular clientele at his restaurant. Moreover, he was able to attend to the basic concerns for food, shelter, and security. I overcompensated by achieving considerable success, security, and autonomy through diligent enterprise. These were not only my battles, but also his that I had to win!

My mother's karma challenged me, too. My mother is a soulful but untreated manic-depressive, susceptible to raging outbursts. Early on, I learned to suspend any expression of feeling for fear of provoking her emotional explosions. Her problem with transforming her powerful impulses haunted me for a long time, only to be resolved somewhat by extensive analytic therapy. At best, my long-term therapy helped me to discover my capacity to transform compulsive instincts into intimacy, albeit in an introverted mode.

As I achieved worldly success and security, I also nourished my patients' hearts and souls. Struggling with my mother's manic depression and mood lability, I learned how to deal with the subtleties of feeling in the intimate encounter of the therapeutic relationship. The unresolved karma of both my parents, though initially burdensome, became the sand around which the oyster of my life has constellated the pearl of my sense of self and individuation, my calling in life as a healer.

Boris Matthews: My Story of Family Karma

The death of my father when I was three years old left my mother having to fend for herself in a part of the country where she indeed had friends but no support from her immediate family. As a single parent supporting herself and her only child during economically difficult times, she was often exhausted and struggled with a depression that probably haunted her all her life. When she was only 18 months old, she lost her mother to blood poisoning when her brother was born. Later, as a widow, she had no one with whom to share intimacy. Her life experiences as well as the economic hardships she had to endure impoverished her capacity to communicate her own needs and feelings, and to venture out assertively on her own. Both she and I shared a compulsion to take care of other people's needs for our own emotional security. When she remarried, I suddenly realized how great an unconscious sense of responsibility I had felt for her. I thought, "I won't have to take care of Mother!" The unconscious imperative to take care of mother (which I did with considerable ambivalence) was one of the factors that I had effectively allowed to block my expression of personal initiative. I also picked up my mother's fear that she would jeopardize her security if she expressed herself by exercising initiative and expressing her views. First, she dreaded provoking her stepmother's retaliation, and, later in life, her employer's, the various school principles and superintendents whom she feared would fire her and replace her with someone more compliant.

For many years, the patterns of attitude, emotion, and behavior (her karmic legacy) that I assumed from my relationship with my mother shaped much of my life. I believed I had to take care of the women I was involved with, starting with the girls I dated in high school. As I became less fearful of offending the woman in my life, I began to be freer to establish more security in my personal and professional life by communicating my needs and ideas.

THE IMPORTANCE OF RELATIONSHIPS TO OUR SOUL GROWTH

Psychoanalyst Heinz Kohut identified three kinds of relationship, or "self-object," experience.[1] These are experiences of relationship with other people (objects of our love) that affirm our sense of self in one way or another. The first of these relationship experiences, in which another affirms the validity of our strivings, secures our soul. The second relationship experience, in which somebody appears to be everything we would like to become, challenges our soul. The third, in which we experience another person as "just like us," befriends our soul. Each of these relationship experiences contributes to our ability to discern and actualize our authentic, innate talents and nature, the "blueprint" of who and what we are: our soul.

Soul

It's important to clarify what we mean by "soul." First, we do not use the word "soul" in the context of any particular religion. Rather, we think of soul as deriving from the Transcendent Source that Itself is the ground from which the various spiritual and religious traditions arise. In fact, our position is that all individual things that manifest in the material world ultimately proceed from the Transcendent Source, the Ground of Being. In our view, soul is the prefiguration, or template, for what takes physical form, as well as what we experience at our human level when our attitudes, emotions, and actions are in accord with that prefiguration. When we're living lives that actualize that template, we feel that we're "in the groove," that we're "getting it right." Hence "soulful" experiences are those in which we consciously are living in accordance with our unique, in-born nature.

All individual things that come into being in the material world are prefigured in soul, hence the importance of relationships that secure, challenge, and befriend the soul.

Relationships that Secure the Soul

A growing infant feels a sense of its value and worth when the parents joyfully accept and celebrate his or her mini-achievements. This is the "mirroring" experience that reflects a child's developing potential. Later in life, the child looks up to parents as strong, powerful, and affirming persons who provide a feeling of safety, security, and freedom to expand his or her frontiers and further explore the world.

Almost all of us get some of this early in life; if we didn't, we would probably not survive infancy, or survive only with serious deficits. To the extent that we do not have loving "mirrors" who accurately and appreciatively reflect who and what we are, we get a distorted view of ourselves. When, as adults, we recognize that we are stuck, that we repeatedly have unfulfilling or painful experiences, we need someone— a friend, a partner, a therapist—who can accurately mirror both the current reality of what we are and our undeveloped potential.

In the course of the mirroring relationship, we change internally as an "inner good parent" develops. As our internal psychological structure changes, we feel differently about ourselves, more positive, less damningly self-critical. We become able to recognize our strengths and good qualities, and trust ourselves in new ways that do not depend on immediate feedback from other people. We become freer.

Journal Exercise: Relationships that Secure My Soul

Open your journal to two facing blank pages. At the top of the left-hand page write "Relationships that Secure My Soul." List all the people over the course of your life who you believe have "seen the real you," who believed in you and affirmed you.

At the top of the right-hand page, write "Relationships that Harm my Soul." Write the names of all the people who have put you down; who didn't appreciate you; who couldn't see the real you.

Then on a separate page for each person, reminisce about that person: how they treated you; how you felt in their presence; how their relationship with you affected you for better or worse. What was special—especially beneficial or detrimental—about them that was and still is so important to you?

Write at the top of a third page "People in My Life Who Mirror My Reality." On separate pages for each of these persons, reflect on the ways each of them sees and affirms your potential; how each of them cares enough about you to lovingly confront you when you fall short of being your best self.

Relationships that Challenge the Soul

"When I grow up, I want to be like . . ." With those words, we identify a goal, an ideal. We all need to be able to idealize something or someone. When we see our ideal realized, it gives us courage to try to do likewise. It proves to us that our ideal is possible in the world in which we live. Of course, our ideals can change over time, and that is natural. Who would want to be a teenager worshiping a popular singer or entertainer or movie star all her or his life?

Whether we have an actual or a fantasy relationship with that idealized person, we feel the urge to of become like her or him. The idealizing relationship can both challenge and motivate us. Whereas the mirroring relationship reflects our current reality and the potential we can further develop, the idealizing relationship shows us the possibility of realizing something that inspires us.

Journal Exercise: Relationships that Challenge My Soul

Open your journal to facing blank pages. At the top of the left-hand page, write "Relationships that Challenge My Soul." Write down the names of all the women and men you've admired and wanted to be like. They may be friends, relatives, public figures, people from history.

Take a separate page in your journal for each of them, and write about the qualities you saw and admired in them that you want to cultivate in yourself. What can you do now to come closer to being like them? What hinders you from becoming more like them?

Relationships that Befriend the Soul

In relationships that befriend the soul, we feel that we and the other person are essentially the same, that is, that we are "twins." (Kohut called these "twinship" relationships.)[2] We trust what our "twin" reflects to us; the distance we experience when we idealize another person vanishes. Both idealizing and twinship relationships energize us, but they feel different.

An idealizing relationship inspires us to strive toward a goal; a twinship relationship vitalizes us as we actually join with another with whom we share an affinity. These are the conditions in which we need relationships that facilitate healing.

Journal Exercise: Relationships that Befriend My Soul

In your journal, make a list of all the people who have felt or feel like your "twin": individuals who are "just like me." (Of course, we realize that they do differ from us in some ways, but the feeling of twinship overrides our knowledge of our differences.)

On a separate page for each person, describe the qualities you have in common. What has resulted from your twinship? How have you grown? What have you accomplished because of your twinship?

When we are fortunate enough to have optimal self-object experiences—relationships that secure, challenge, and befriend our soul, either as infants, children, or in adult life—we increasingly trust our own emerging potential. Then we develop a vital, creative, and joyful sense of self. The acorn is on the way to becoming the oak tree in such fertile psychological soil. If, on the other hand, we lack these experiences, our psyche sustains deep wounds that may take several generations to heal. Some of us are fortunate to get a second chance at such healing self-object experiences in a significant relationship: with a partner, friend, mentor, or therapist.

By assessing the stories of our grandparents we get a deeper understanding of our self-object experiences, of the family complexes and myths into which we have been born, and what might be our dharmic task, the calling of our soul. An additional framework that may facilitate understanding our family karma is our parents' choice of godparents for us, and our choice of mentors. We hypothesize that our parents may unconsciously choose godparents that complement but more often compensate for the missing piece of psyche from them and from our grandparents. In early adulthood, we may then choose mentors who help us overcome personal or family karmic obstacles and fill in more gaps in our development.

Godparents and mentors gives us a significant clue as to what part of our grandparental karma we need to retire and what was missing from our self-object experiences in our family. In gaining such clues, we may not only retire the family karma, but often stumble into our dharma, our soul's calling, our life's task. If this is not the outcome, then at the very least, retiring the family karma of our ancestors clears the way for attending to our dharma, our individuation, our soul work in this lifetime.

Ashok Bedi's Visit with Mayor Giuliani

I was in a creativity block for a few days as I was pondering the theme of family karma. My tape recorder broke, the battery for the new one was dead, and I could not formulate any thoughts on family karma. I was incubating the idea that family karma might be nothing but working though the parental complexes. This seemed like "Analysis 101," and I was not sure if the concept of family karma had anything new to add to the mix. Yet intuitively I knew that there was a subtle and significant theme that begged to be delineated. In this mind frame, I had the following dream that unlocked the crucial aspect of my family karma:

> *I am at my grandparents' home in India, in a musty old room, and I have a meeting with Mayor Rudolph Giuliani of New York City. He recently had a negative TV piece on inappropriate campaign practices in which a liberal young man expressed some concerns about his campaign methods. Initially, I am oppositional to the mayor, but he is poised and respectful of my views and soon I find myself cataloguing his many civic contributions including the improved law and order in the big city. Then I start telling him about my dead grandfather and he respectfully listens to me. I find myself both criticizing and honoring my grandfather in the communication. The dream ends at this point.*

As I analyzed this dream, it became apparent to me that it held the answer to my riddle about family karma.

Our parents and parental complexes shape our ego complex, our adaptation to our outer life, our maya strivings. Identification with or opposition to parental personalities forms and shapes our personalities and the way we attend to personal and professional realms in the early part of life. However, in the second half of life, it is often our grandparents and our family history that sets the stage of our deeper and higher strivings. The unfinished business of our grandparents becomes the dharmic quest.

My great-grandfather, Guru Nanak, was the founder of the Sikh religion and wrote the initial parts of the holy text of Sikhs, the *Guru Granth Sahib*, the Holy Book. In his rendering of Sikh faith, he emphasized the integrative aspects of Hindu and Muslim tenets. My on-going dharmic task has been and continues to be integrating the Eastern and Western philosophies toward a holistic understanding of the human condition and soul work. While I am no Guru Nanak, I am humbled to learn that in a small way I am carrying on the tradition of my family. I am continuing to build the bridge between traditions: Christian and Hindu, medical and psychoanalytic, outer and inner.

Viewed from this perspective of family karma, the grandparents, godparents, and mentors assume considerable significance in our psychic landscape. They often set the tone for our second half of life, for our dharmic quest. It is as if our parental complexes and the opus of the first half of our life may be a preparation phase for the magnum opus of the second half of our life.

Journal Exercise: Filling in the Gaps

In this exercise, we want you to remember and think about the gaps in your mentoring, and the people who failed as well as those who have mentored you in ways your parents didn't or couldn't. Title this first page "Failed Mentors." Starting with your parents, grandparents, and other close relatives, list those who did not mentor you, whom you looked to for instruction and support, but were unable or unwilling to provide it. On a separate page for each of them, discuss where they let you down, what their limitations were, how you believe they failed you.

On a fresh page in your journal titled "True Mentors," write the names of all those people who have taken a special interest in helping you become who you potentially can be, the people who "filled in the gaps." These people are your mentors: grandparents, godparents, teachers in school or college, neighbors, family friends, relatives, colleagues, etc.

On a separate page for each mentor, recollect how he or she influenced you. What did they help you achieve? How was their style of mentoring especially beneficial? How are they echoed in your life now?

Who are your mentors now? How are they helping you become more fully who you truly are? What are you learning from them?

Now we are going to share with you several case histories from our psychotherapy practices. We have, of course, changed the names and some details to protect the confidentiality of our clients. As you read these case vignettes, keep in mind the kinds of relationships that secure, challenge, and befriend the soul, as well as what you discovered as you worked through the journal exercises earlier in this chapter. See if you can identify what each of the persons in the following stories did not get but needed to live their authentic life potential.

The Tyranny of Marlene's Grandfather

Marlene's grandfather was a rough-and-tumble "man's man": proficient in sports, who talked to his buddies for hours about football, baseball, hunting, fishing, and sundry "masculine" activities, but who failed as a mentor for his son, Marlene's father. The "feminine" and aesthetic dimension was prominent in its absence from his psyche. Marlene's father was the opposite of her grandfather. He enjoyed aesthetic pursuits: playing the piano, listening to music, collecting art and antique furniture. He was ill-at-ease in all-male company, but could painfully fake it to get by.

Marlene was raised like a boy and was more at home in a masculine environment. She was uncomfortable in her feminine role, but the feminine aspects of her psyche kept calling her to assimilate her inner femininity and live out the outer feminine in relationship. As she was struggling with this issue, she had the following dream, which was the answer to the riddle of her soul work.

There is this old mansion. I've dreamed about it many times. The city has sort of grown up around it, and forgotten it is there. I've been there sometimes. You have to crawl through underbrush and brambles to get to it. I've seen it from the outside, but have never been inside. I've always tried to imagine what it would be like to *live there, and I've always believed it was intended for me. Now the old lady living there is going to rent out an apartment. I am with a group of people who now get to see the inside. I'm excited. But when I get in, I'm stunned to find out that she has already rented it to my father! For $1,000 a month! I had always thought it was meant for me, but now I realize it is perfect for my father, and was always intended for him. His apartment is beautiful: beautiful old antique furniture that he loved, art on the walls, books and bookcases. It's what he would have had if he had not married and taken on the responsibilities of a family. The old woman's part of the mansion has lots and lots of rooms. Each room is full of stuff. All kinds of things. Some of it seems worthless. She has collected everything for years—maybe hundreds of years. But some of the things she has are rare and valuable if you can recognize them.*

Talking about the dream, Marlene said that the old woman was very old, maybe hundreds of years old. Every room was full of stuff. A lot of people would never notice what she had. Some articles were worthless, but then you'd see something very valuable.

As a young man, her father had collected a few pieces of antique furniture that Marlene remembered. Her father had cherished them, but he had gotten into financial difficulties by overspending for antiques. He wanted to play the piano; he was great at interior decorating, much better than her mother. He had fine taste. Yet, at family gatherings he was uncomfortable when the men watched football games or discussed sports. It was painful to see him trying to take part in those conversations.

Marlene realized that she and her mother had always believed they had to make up for those aspects of masculinity that her father lacked. After the dream, Marlene felt both relieved and disoriented. She realized that she had attempted to live her father's unintegrated masculinity. "Who am I now?" she asked herself. "I'm not sure I really want to have those antiques and those works of art to take care of. I feel lighter, unburdened. Something's opening up for me. Maybe I'll be able to explore more feminine things now."

The dream unlocks the mystery of Marlene's problems, and gives her a key to resolving the central issue. It seems that one major dynamic in Marlene's story was that she was caught in her grandfather's family karma. Her grandfather was "all male," inside and out, and was disconnected from the aesthetic, creative, and feminine aspects of his soul. Her father then had to live out grandfather's unlived feminine by his interest in arts and aesthetics. For her part, Marlene was caught in a bind: she had developed a strong intellect, but also felt some obligation to preserve many of her father's treasures in her own home.

In the dream, the archetypal Great Mother shows her rooms and rooms full of treasures that she can select from at her heart's desire, something she thought she had always wanted to do. But to her surprise, she finds out in the dream that the old woman has already rented the rooms to her father. Then the awakening comes: the feeling of relief: All those antiques are her father's way of expressing the archetypal feminine, but not hers! She feels liberated to explore other ways of experiencing and living the archetypal feminine, ways more in accord with her innate potential. Her dream "broke the karmic spell" cast by her grandfather's one-sided masculinity and her father's attempt to compensate for it.

The Tyranny of Howard's Grandmother

Howard had been in therapy several times over the years. When he came for therapy, he was on leave from his ministry, seriously contemplating leaving the clergy. All his 30 years as a minister, he had been involved with people as a teacher, mentor, or administrator. He had always felt his worth as a human being depended on his doing something important: helping people, or being involved in some worthy project. Now on leave and working a 9-to-5 business office job, he felt both relief that he didn't have to take his job home with him, and a deep unrest tinged with feelings of guilt that he wasn't doing something "important."

In his many years in the clergy, he had traveled extensively. Travel—or the prospect of travel—had been exciting: one week in this city, the next week in another, or arranging tours or even leading the faithful on trips to the Holy Land. Now, in his quiet way of life, he longed for the excitement that travel had provided. Yet, as he reflected on his many journeys, he remembered that when he arrived in a city, he often felt lonely; and after he had finished his assignment there, he would drive or fly off to another city, only to repeat the experience of anticipation, work, and the distressing sensation of emptiness and meaninglessness. But, he told himself, regardless how he felt, he was doing something important for people and furthering the work of his denomination.

Howard's decision to enter the clergy was deeply embedded in the karma of his family. One karmic strand came from Howard's father who had never achieved his dream of farming his own land, but had barely been able to support his family as a tenant or sharecropper. Howard's family had been desperately poor; his parents were always deeply distressed about money. From early on, Howard had often walked in the woods, weeping, longing to escape the brutal, depressing, poverty-stricken existence. He remembered that his father had, a few times, been playful with him and the other children. But that had been the exception. When Howard was about 17, his father realized he would never be able to have his own farm. The death of his dream soon led to his father's physical death. For Howard, his father's death was a major marker: before Dad died, and after Dad died. But by that time, Howard had been in a church school for four years, spending only the summers working on the farm, and enduring the silent reproaches of his brothers who had not yet escaped, as he had, to boarding school.

A different strand of family karma had led Howard to attend the denominational high school and study for the clergy. When he was six or seven, Howard's maternal grandmother had begun to exert a strong, constant influence on him. His grandmother was one of several children from a large immigrant family who had left Austria rather than serve in the Austrian Imperial Army. His great-grandfather had established himself successfully, and although not well-to-do, was prosperous and respected in his community. However, Howard's grandmother and great-grandfather had often been in conflict, so much so that Grandmother had come both to distrust men and, to ensure her safety, to control them.

What linked Grandmother and Howard was her deep disappointment when her son, Howard's uncle, stopped going to church, in part because of his loss of faith upon witnessing the atrocities of WWII in Europe. Howard's uncle had always been independent-minded; Grandmother could not make him return to the fold. When Grandmother visited, she always led Howard's family in reading the Bible, praying that her son would be led back to the church. Howard realized that she had strongly influenced him in his decision to study for the ministry. By becoming a minister, he would both "make up for" his uncle's lapse of faith as well as escape the desperate life as a hired hand on some other man's farm.

But the clergy had not assuaged the gnawing emptiness Howard had experienced throughout his childhood, adolescence, and adult life. He realized that he had tried to fill the void with the excitement of work and travel. But that had not worked. He recognized that he longed for his father. After we had explored his life-long father hunger, Howard paid a visit to his uncle, something he had hesitated to do because he had been unable to fully accept that during his many years in the clergy he had not been living an authentic life.

Howard's visit initiated a significant transformation in his view of himself and the degree of self-acceptance. The uncle welcomed Howard. Because he had had the courage to follow the prompting of his soul and had picked himself up and carried on after reverses in fortune, Howard's uncle understood something of what Howard was going through. Howard began to realize that, without knowing it, he had tried to live a life that would relieve his grandmother's guilt over her son's leaving the church. When her son refused to fulfill her desires, Grandmother found in six-year-old Howard a boy longing for attention and affection whom she could influence and thereby assuage her guilt.

With insight into his family karma, Howard is more comfortable with his choice to leave the clergy. He is beginning to realize more fully that the excitement he used to pursue failed to fill his emptiness. As he struggles with the idea that he should be doing something "important," he is cultivating friendships that offer what his "important" activities of the past failed to do. In a word, Howard is realizing that "being" must be the foundation for "doing;" then life can be good.

Howard was living out Grandmother's family karma. Her desire to live a spiritual life, though laudable, was, for Howard, a tyranny that engulfed his uncle's and his own life. And yet it was the grandson who broke the grip of this tyrannical hold on the family by making a decision to live a more authentic life: perhaps not "religious" in the formal sense that his Grandmother would have liked, but deeply religious by honoring the calling of his soul.

Alexandra's Dance with Her Ancestors' Suffering

One day, Alexandra brought a seemingly simple dream to therapy: *I received an invitation to the dance!* Alexandra loved to dance, but said she was not a good dancer unless her partner could lead well. Alexandra said that on awaking she knew that the invitation was to the "dance of intimacy." We hoped she would get another dream that would tell us more what the dance was about.

In a subsequent session, Alexandra indeed brought another dance dream:

> *I am dancing with Peter. He is an excellent dancer. At one point, we fall down, but get back up again and continue to dance as though nothing has happened.*

Alexandra's personal suffering started with being born into a family of Russian descent. As with many Russian immigrant families from the Soviet Union, Alexandra experienced many tensions in her childhood. The death of Alexandra's mother (at age 40) was a great tragedy for her and her sister. Their father had to support the family; Alexandra and her sister had to take care of the house and of each other. Alexandra's grandparents had both been sent to Siberia, supposedly for subversive political activity.

Alexandra said that Peter had Russian ancestry, as did she. He had spent his childhood in an orphanage. Alexandra could relate to his personal pain, because her mother had died mysteriously when Alexandra was in grade school. Peter, Alexandra said, suffered the agony of his Russian ancestry. So did Alexandra. They had a deep understanding of each other that neither needed to verbalize.

As an adult, married woman, Alexandra valued education as the ticket to a better life. She and her husband were able to provide their children better opportunities and much more family stability than Alexandra and her parents had experienced. But Alexandra did not forget her painful childhood, nor the toll it extracted from her. She chose to work with unmarried mothers living in the city, women who had often abused alcohol and drugs, and had many children. Each of the families she worked with was on the edge of desperation, but Alexandra continued to visit them, continued to hope for them, continued to encourage and support, but often with only meager successes.

Her own family beginnings and the desperate families she worked with were very much like many of the first generation Russian immigrants to the U.S.: forced to live in ghettos, barely able to make ends meet, plagued by alcohol abuse.

We were still puzzled, however. What were these two dreams telling us that we didn't already know?

When we considered them together, we realized that Alexandra was being invited to dance with her personal and ancestral suffering. It was an "invitation." "Invitation" was a word that carried a great significance for Alexandra, a word often used in the spiritual reading she had been sharing with friends. Together these two dreams appeared to show Alexandra that her spiritual calling (the "invitation") was to dance with her personal and ancestral karma of the suffering Russian people. The burden was so heavy that she would sometimes fall down, and that was part of it, but that she could and would always be able to get up again and continue dancing as though nothing had happened.

The dream invited Alexandra to assimilate her personal, family, and ethnic suffering into a legacy of courage and survival. She moved from being a victim to being a survivor, and ultimately to a mode of mastery over her destiny. Her dream was the calling of her soul.

Although it is sometimes difficult to trace, the karma of our family often reaches back more than two generations. Not only our parents and grandparents, but our great-grandparents and their parents contribute to family patterns that shape our lives.

In the next chapter, we will explore the seven traditional kundalini chakras as morphogenic fields that can carry family karma. When one or more of our chakras has been strongly influenced by an ancestral morphogenic field, we face the task of balancing the affected chakras. When we have done that, we have a better chance of pursuing our authentic path, our individuation.

5

HOW WE INHERIT FAMILY KARMA: COMPLEXES, MORPHOGENIC FIELDS, AND THE CHAKRAS

Carl Jung observed family karma when he wrote: "Children are so deeply involved in the psychological attitude of their parents that it is no wonder that most of the nervous disturbances in childhood can be traced back to a disturbed psychic atmosphere in the home."[1] For successful but one-sided parents, this sometimes implies that their children suffer their parents' unconscious darkness. The children of unsuccessful or disabled parents may feel compelled to actualize their parents' unrealized potential. This explains in part why children of unsuccessful parents succeed in many areas of life where their parents failed whereas children of some successful parents are often susceptible to drug abuse, relationship problems, and other difficulties in living.

Moreover, Jung wrote, "For all lovers of theory, the essential fact behind all this is that the things which have the most powerful effect upon children do not come from the conscious state of the parents but from their unconscious background."[2] In other words, the children often carry the burden of their ancestors' unconscious lives: both their unlived potential and unrecognized shadow. What do we mean by "unconscious"?

THE UNCONSCIOUS

Actually, we don't know for sure what the unconscious is. The best we can say is that the unconscious is everything going on in you of which you are unaware. In other words, the unconscious is the psychic unknown: all those experiences, memories, ideas, influences, and forces that at the moment are "out of mind" but that nevertheless affect you in some way are part of the unconscious.

But this way of speaking is somewhat misleading: putting it like this implies that the unconscious is a "something," like the stomach or liver, that we only notice when it acts up and causes us pain. Actually, it is we who are unconscious of it, this psychic unknown in which we are imbedded and that besets us with dreams, moods, intuitions, and fantasies, as well as punctures our inflated states, reducing us again to human size. The psychic unknown—the unconscious—is involved in our individual karma, both influencing our actions and dealing out some of the consequences of our actions.

The notion of something unconscious is important in considering the dynamics of karma. A great deal goes on in our body-psyche that usually does not enter our daytime, waking consciousness. We are unconscious of much that is happening in us all the time. Fantasies and dreams are evidence that our waking consciousness is not the whole of who we are. In waking life, sometimes we make slips of the tongue, saying something we felt strongly but didn't want to mention. Or we resolve to undertake a task we don't want to do, only to discover that we do it at the wrong time, make errors, miss the deadline, or totally forget it. Something in us cooperates with our gut feeling, even though we have made up our mind to override our gut. This "something" is what we call "the unconscious."

Often we inherit the ancestral layer of karma unconsciously. Let's look at some of the ways that family karma is transmitted unconsciously.

FAMILY COMPLEXES AND THE
WORD-ASSOCIATION EXPERIMENTS

Early in the 20th century, Jung discovered that complexes run in families. Complexes (see pages 119–126 for further discussion of complexes) are clusters of memories, experiences, places, and characteristics that are held together by a common emotion. Whenever we experience any one or two elements in such a cluster, they can elicit the emotion that holds them all together and we feel as though we are again experiencing the situation that originally formed the complex. Our current language refers to this phenomenon by saying that we "go ballistic," that our "buttons have been pushed." Jung made this discovery while he was working with the word-association experiment.

The word-association experiment consists of a list of 100 common words, such as mother, home, school, work, etc. The experimenter reads the words one at a time to the test subject who responds with the first thing that comes to mind. For example, one person responded to the word "dear" by saying "child." Another stimulus word was "family," and his response was "many people." The experimenter measures the subject's response time. Then the experimenter goes through the entire list a second time. In doing this, Jung noticed two things. First, that some reaction times were significantly different—shorter or longer than the average reaction time. Second, when he repeated the experiment, he saw that the subject was able to reproduce the original response except in those instances where the reaction time was shorter or longer than the mean. This led Jung to the realization that something in the subject's psyche was interfering with the responses. Jung called this "something" the "feeling-toned complex."[3]

Later in his experimental researches, Jung discovered that members of the same family often revealed similar patterns in their responses to the same stimulus words, implying that members of the family had some similar complexes. In other words, family members often reacted with the same emotions to similar situations. Table 1 on page 54 reproduces some of the associations of a mother and her daughter from one of Jung's experiments.[4]

From this brief example we can see that mother and daughter share several emotional responses. As Jung observes, "The daughter shares her mother's way of thinking, not only in her ideas but also in her forms of expression; so much so that she even uses the same

Table 1. Word Associations of a Mother and Her Daughter.

Stimulus Word	Mother	Daughter
Law	God's commandment	Moses
Strange	Traveler	Travelers
A burn	Great pain	Painful
Door	Wide	Big
Coal	Sooty	Black
Fruit	Sweet	Sweet

words. . . . If, therefore, even the most superficial and apparently most fleeting mental images are entirely due to the constellation of the environment, what must we not expect for the more important mental activities, for emotions, wishes, hopes, and intentions?"[5]

According to Jung, parental complexes have a molding influence on the developing character of the child. Some children will imitate the parent, developing a similar complex even though the child has not had the life experiences that contributed to the development of the parent's complexes. Here, the karma of the complex is passed on by parental example. But the subtler influences operate outside of conscious awareness.

What most influences the child are the unconscious, personal affective states—the emotional component of the complex—of the parents and teachers. People sometimes express affective states without realizing that they are, even though we can recognize they are gripped by an emotion. But it also happens that people repress strong emotions that nevertheless affect others.

People who repress strong emotions create a certain kind of atmosphere around them. They don't seem to be quite real, or it's hard to trust them emotionally, or we don't feel fully safe in their presence. We can't tell what is going on in them, yet their very presence causes discomfort. How is it possible that their repressed emotion affects us?

Emotions are a form of energy that we experience in our body. A repeated emotion—such as fear—appears to create an enduring force field that pulls us in one direction or another. For example, someone who is angry emits a force field that we feel in our gut as a sensation that we may identify as anger or fear. In the presence of a person who is sexually aroused, we may feel a corresponding sexual energy. Someone else may be very much in the head, and we can sense that we also get "heady," or feel "ungrounded." These are examples of force fields that have been identified in the system of kundalini yoga as chakras.

MORPHOGENIC FIELDS
AND THE KUNDALINI CHAKRAS

Energy fields exist in many forms. Perhaps the best-known analogy to a morphogenic field is that of the magnet.[6] In high school science class, we took a bar magnet or horseshoe magnet, laid a piece of glass over it, and sprinkled iron filings on the glass. The filings flowed into the characteristic pattern of curves, thereby revealing the force field of the magnet. The magnet exerts a field of energy that generates a certain shape, hence the name, *morpho* ("shape") *genic* ("forming"). Now, if we bring a stronger magnet near the first magnet and the pattern of iron filings, we will see the pattern begin to shift. The stronger field dominates and distorts the original field. This is a fair analogy of what happens in intimate relationships and family systems: the dominant member exerts a formative, and sometimes distorting, influence on younger and weaker family members who are in their formative stages.

The subtle energy of a morphogenic field organizes form, such as behavior and attitude. Energies likewise radiate from a person who is experiencing a strong emotion. Often we can resonate with the specific emotion another person is feeling, which can be either a pleasant or uncomfortable sensation. When families live in close proximity, sometimes for generations, what impact do they have on each other? How do the more dominant members, e.g., parents, impact their children physically, psychologically and karmicly? As we discussed earlier, Jung found from his experiments with word association that the complexes of parents entangle their children in similar complexes,[7] even though the children did not have the formative experiences that created their parent's complexes. We understand Jung's findings to imply that the parents generated emotional fields, perhaps very subtle as well as consciously perceptible, that shaped or formed their children's emotional lives. In other words, the parents produced emotional morphogenic fields. The parental morphogenic fields established a template, as it were, that organized similar emotions and emotional reactions in their children. Once a morphogenic field is established, it persists; that is, a morphogenic field does not need a physical embodiment to continue to exist. Rather, it exists "in the air," as it were. The morphogenic field hypothesis would account for the enduring quality of habits, as well as for the difficulty of discovering or inventing new ways of feeling and behaving.

We further hypothesize that the seven primary Kundalini chakras may be very ancient morphogenic fields. Most people have experienced the third Kundalini chakra as the "fire in the belly." That burning sensation in the belly may correspond to enthusiasm, drive, anger, or fear. Emotions, behaviors, and attitudes are associated with each of the other six chakras. When each chakra is balanced (i.e., neither over- or under-energized), and all seven are in balance with one another, we have attained an optimal physical, emotional, mental, and spiritual state. Needless to say, most of us are still working toward this goal. However, when one or more of the chakras is far out of balance, that chakra disharmony creates unbalanced chakric fields that affect other people.

From our emerging understanding of the chakras, we hypothesize that parents who are stuck in one or more of their chakras exert a compelling influence on their children. Clinical evidence supports the hypothesis that, in such instances, it becomes the burden of the vulnerable children to retire the family karma of the parent's chakra imbalance before they can attain their own kundalini balance.

FAMILY LEGACY IN THE SEVEN CHAKRAS

In the system of yoga, the chakras—subtle energy centers—shape mind, soul, and body. Each of the seven chakras, in its own way, is responsible for a certain level of growth of spiritual awareness, psycho-emotional development, and physical health and well-being. The seven primary chakras are situated along the length of the spine.[8] Each individual's destiny in selfhood lies in attaining consciousness and balance among the seven chakras.

As focal points where physical, emotional, and spiritual dimensions of our being intersect, each chakra inherits the morphic field legacy of family karma from parents, grandparents, and earlier ancestors. That legacy may be a blessing or a curse; but it is our inheritance, and it serves or saddles us. We must each deal with the karma that our family has accumulated, because the inertia of that karma will tend to handicap us with problems not of our personal making as well as with "blessings" that may push us beyond our innate limits.

The first three chakras—root, sacral, and solar plexus—are responsible for survival, sense of self, and inner power, respectively. The fourth chakra, the heart center, is the point where we can transform self-centered instincts and inner impulses into feelings and actions that take others, and ultimately, the universal reality into account. This begins the movement from limited reality ("maya") toward experiencing the interconnectedness of all being. The last three chakras—throat, third eye, and crown—are universal centers, focusing on communication, insight, and wholeness.

Caroline Shola Arewa has a beautiful way of writing about the chakras and what they mean:

> The chakras are like a ladder on which we can climb up to the clouds—this is our expansion—or down to earth—our limita-

tion. Each rung has a different lesson. We can get stuck in one place—up high, unable to see down, or down low, unable to see above us. We may have no knowledge of the ladder and the opportunity it affords. Some rungs may be wobbly and therefore a bit scary to climb. One side may be stronger, so we may avoid the weak side and step confidently only to the left feminine or right masculine.[9]

Stepping left or right refers to the two channels—assertive ("masculine") and receptive ("feminine")—that crisscross as they wind their way up the spinal column around the seven chakras. Within each of the seven chakras, a person could live in the assertive channel or in the receptive channel. However, that would be relatively unbalanced. The goal of a life that fulfills the soul's potential, or dharma, is gradually to attain balance and centering in the dominant chakra, and development of the optimal balance in the remaining six chakras.

In order to establish balance among your chakras, you need to recognize the areas of your life where you are either too energized or too yielding, and take the actions that will balance the relevant chakras. This kind of unbalanced condition may have developed because of family patterns—morphogenic fields—that have affected one or more of your chakras.

The table on pages 60–61 summarizes the chakras and the psychospiritual stage each governs.

The first chakra emphasizes the need for survival and security. The second governs erotic drive and generativity. The third chakra focuses the quest for power, control, and authority. The fourth, heart chakra, transforms instincts and drives into feelings and relatedness. The fifth, throat chakra, sponsors finding your own voice in this world. The sixth, "third eye," chakra is concerned with development of intuition, wisdom and leadership. And the seventh, the crown chakra, relates to individuation, liberation, and your quest for union with the divine. Each chakra operates in a balanced or unbalanced natural state. But with proper physical and spiritual exercises and disciplines we can transform each chakra from its natural state to a spiritually evolved one. In this book, we focus on balancing the natural state, but we will mention the evolved condition of the sixth and seventh chakras.

Each one of us is inherently most at home in one of these seven chakras. Yet you must be able to access the energy and the guidance of all the seven chakras as the task at hand demands. In our clinical experience, we have found that people often get stuck in a chakra other than their primary one due to the force of their family karma. This discrepancy between the natural, primary chakra, and the family-imposed chakra creates a tension that results in neurosis, relationship problems, medical and psychiatric illness, accidents, and under-performance in critical areas of love, work, play, creativity, and spirituality. The task is, first, to recognize where ancestral patterns have over-energized one or more chakras; and, second, to reset the chakra balance.

Parents and children often form two-person or three-person chakric fields. Actually, we all do this to some greater or lesser extent with all the persons emotionally close to us. When parents are living too much either in their assertive or their receptive channels, they create unbalanced morphogenic chakra fields in the family. The parental morphogenic fields create emotional imbalance in the chakras of the developing child. The child attempts to respond by one of the only two means available to it: it either carries the compensatory channel for the imbalanced parent, or joins the parent in the imbalance.

For example, if the father is stuck in the assertive channel, the daughter may carry the receptive channel for that particular chakra. This would be the daughter's attempt to heal the imbalanced chakric field. Alternatively, if the environment is too threatening to the child's psyche, he or she may identify with the parent's dominant emotional field and channel (e.g., identify with the aggressor). Either of these options serves psychic survival, both of the fragile parent and the vulnerable child. The child is thus diverted from a growth mode to a survival mode. Often adults finally recognize that they have been leading unauthentic lives, reacting to "invisible" parental presence.

Table 2. Chakra Overview.

Chakra	Main Function	Developmental Task	Unbalanced Roles
7. Crown	Wholeness, liberation	Individuation; selfless-ness; union with Higher Power; fulfillment	Social isolationist, narcissist vs. megalomaniac
6. Brow	Wisdom; inner vision	Intuition, inner wisdom	Mental slave, unquestioning follower vs. dogmatist; dictatorial leader, abuser of higher powers
5. Throat	Power of Communication	Power of the creative word; awareness of and communication with spirit; ability to sense and attune to energy	Masked/disconnected self vs. intimidator, demagogue
4. Heart	Transition from embodiment to enlightenment	Transform compulsive instincts into related intimacy	Caretaker/co-dependent/devourer vs. performer
3. Solar Plexus	Personal power and enthusiasm	Self-assertion, effectiveness, vitality and energy	Drudge/slave vs. tyrant/dictator
2. Sacral	Sense of Self	Love and trust in self and one's instincts	Martyr vs. exploiter
1. Root	Embodiment	Basic survival and grounding	Victim vs. aggressor

Table 2. Chakra Overview. (Cont.)

Balanced Roles	Unbalanced Emotions	Balanced Emotions
Spiritual master; spiritual elder	Disorientation; constant worry; fragmentation; megalomania	Peak experience; peace; oneness
Guru; wise person; seer	Skepticism; cynicism; spiritual inflation	Contentment; stillness of mind & body
Communicator and listener at subtle levels	Restlessness; anxiety; inhibited creativity; verbosity; domination of others	Peacefulness and harmony; stillness;
Lover	Isolation; relatedness	Compassion; selfless love
Warrior	Controlled by emotions: unfeeling, uncaring, quick-tempered, violent, despairing, depressed	Experience and express all emotions easily and appropriately: joy, happiness, passion, rage, sadness, conflict
Sovereign	Fear of emotions and instincts; low self-esteem; or driven by instincts	All instincts permitted without excess; joy in self-expression and body awareness
Embodied and grounded; earth mother/father	Fearful, needy, anxious; bullying, controlling, rigid	Safe, secure, grounded, "alive"; accepting of physical limitations

The subtle nuances of parental moods, conflicts, strengths, behaviors, hang-ups, and interactional styles thus become the building blocks of the child's evolving psychic structures. What happens in the family room, at the breakfast table, on the playground, and in countless significant and mundane exchanges between children and parents becomes the defining lines in the child's destiny.

In the following, we will present and discuss examples of family karma in each of the seven chakras. In each example, family karma creates an imbalance—a problem—in the chakra under discussion. The chakra impacted by family karma may be the dominant chakra, though this is not always the case. Once the individual retires the family karma in the affected chakra, he or she opens the way to attend to the innately primary chakra and his or her soul's authentic tasks.

For the sake of simplicity, we do not discuss the further individuation of the men and women in our case examples once they have retired the family karma of the chakra under discussion. Most of these individuals have moved on, resuming their soul's journey, and have been able to focus more consciously on their dominant chakra, thus actualizing more of their true potential. For many of these individuals, their soul work is in progress and the mystery of their soul's code continues to unfold on the stage of their life.

FIRST-CHAKRA FAMILY KARMA: TOM'S HORROR OF INSECURITY

Tom is in his 50s, an extremely wealthy, retired businessman, a self-made multimillionaire. Tom has been very successful but is a controlling type of individual who came for therapy and analysis. His presenting problems were his relationship with his son, as well as difficulties with other important people in his life.

Tom's father was professionally unsuccessful. The family was raised in a situation of financial deprivation, always scraping the bottom, sometimes on welfare. As Tom was growing up, he vowed to himself never to let his children experience hardship, degradation, and suffering because of financial need. By the time he was in his 50s, he had built a successful business empire and retired. He set up a trust fund for his son and worked hard at teaching him the skills that had helped him survive in his competitive business environment. His son's trust was due to be dissolved when his son turned 30; then his son would assume control of the funds that his father had set aside for him.

The son started a somewhat ill-conceived business. In spite of Tom's best efforts to protect, guide, and control his son's venture, the son ran the business into the ground and was near bankruptcy by the time Tom came for therapy. Paradoxically, after reviewing the situation, my recommendation was that Tom detach from his son's business enterprise, be emotionally present to his son and available for business consultation if his son so requested, but essentially inform his son that he would honor whatever decision he made about his business.

It was difficult for Tom to let go. As he had initially predicted, his son continued in his imprudent ways, and ran the business further into the ground, depleting most of the trust's assets. Then, surprisingly, on the brink of bankruptcy the son somehow turned the situation around, reorganized his business, and established a much more functional operation with a moderate degree of success.

You may have may concluded that Tom's unsuccessful father was a man who did not have survival and security skills. In other words, he had a first-chakra problem of survival. Raised in this milieu, Tom's first chakra became the top priority, which Tom successfully managed through unmitigated ambition. This kind of drive—a "fire in the belly"—centers in the third chakra of control and authority. Not only did Tom free himself from the financial hardships he grew up in, he was keen to insulate his children and grandchildren from ever having to experience the vicissitudes of survival, and had set up handsome trusts for them.

However, in doing so, he also insulated his children from the experience of the first chakra: developing the skill of survival on the solid ground of Mother Earth, the skill of planting a small seed and helping it grow into a flowering plant that bears some fruit, and provides some shade and security under which we can get life's essentials. Having been devoid of first-chakra experience, Tom's son started to sabotage his business. The son's unconscious motivation was to feel the floor, the ground under his feet, the realities of life. Since there was no way to experience life's imperatives without first removing the safety net and the magic shoes his father had put on his feet, he had to remove those artificial shoes so that he could get his bare feet on solid ground. For him, unfortunately, this meant stripping away the comforts of the trust, the security of his father's business empire, and experiencing his own earth. Only then could he honor his first chakra and rebound on his own, not his father's, terms. When Tom moved out of the way, gradually his son was able to experience the first chakra for himself, get his bearings, and slowly recoup, having now established himself in his own way, and in his own context in his first chakra.

Paradoxically, survival and security problems of the first chakra are often the family legacy of the first-generation rich and famous. In their misguided desire to protect their offspring from the suffering they have endured, they often isolate their children from the experience of Mother Earth and the realities of daily existence that are essential in building lives on a secure foundation. Although these parents have found their footing in the world, in their attempt to protect, they fail to pass on the legacy of the Earth under their feet to their own children.

Characteristics of the First Chakra

Our sense of survival and security rests in the root, or first, chakra. It is our foundation for life. The view of the world from the root chakra is of "uninspired materialism, governed by 'hard facts.' . . . There is on this plane no zeal for life, no explicit impulse to expand. There is simply a lethargic avidity in hanging on to existence. . . ."[10] This chakra, also referred to as the support chakra, is located between the anus and the genitals. Symbolically, it is represented by a square surrounded by four petals. It is governed by the element earth, and its totem animal is the elephant. Fortunately, most of us have evolved somewhat beyond the root chakra, and have some energy for other things besides hanging on to life and survival. Hence, when our root chakra is optimally developed, we are "down to earth," grounded, embodied, steadfast, stable. We have a sense of trust in ourselves, in others, and in the world. We are full of energy and life, structured and organized, and accept our limitations.

When the assertive channel of our root chakra is too strong, we tend to be overly aggressive, self-centered, possessive, controlling, and sometimes anxious and/or fear-dominated. We seek to ensure our survival more or less regardless of other considerations or other people. When the receptive channel of our root chakra is too strong, we end up feeling we're the victim: needy, unmotivated, disorganized, and restricted. When these two energies are balanced in the first chakra, we feel safe, secure, vital; we have the experience of being grounded, adequately mothered, and can mother others and ourselves. We experience disturbances in the first chakra medically as problems in the rectum and genitals; we may suffer from lower back pain, sciatica, and depression.

Journal Exercise: Your Root Chakra

This is the first of seven chakra exercises. Each chakra exercise has several parts. Work through each of the six categories in the chakra chart, referring to Table 2 as necessary.

A: Main Function and Developmental Task

The main function of the first or root chakra is embodiment, and the developmental task is that of fully living in your body and experiencing life not only in you head but in the rest of your physical being. Feeling safe and knowing you are going to survive further characterize the experience of this chakra.

• Describe how you feel about your personal survival.

- In what situations do you most intensely experience the reality of living in your body?
- What are situations in which you feel ungrounded, "blown away," "disembodied," that you might not survive?
- What experiences have changed your sense of embodiment and grounding over time?

B: Role Balance

The possible roles governed by the root chakra range from that of victim through the balanced roles of well-grounded Earth Mother or Earth Father to ruthless aggressor intent on surviving at all costs.

- In general, where do you see yourself on the role spectrum from victim to aggressor?
- In what situations do you feel you are a victim?
- What situations bring out the aggressor intent on survival at all costs?
- In what areas of your life do you recognize that you need to work on your role balance? Intimate relationships? Work? Family of origin?

C: Emotional State and Balance

When your first chakra energies are balanced, you feel safe, secure, grounded, alive in your body, but also accepting of physical limitations. The unbalanced emotions range from fearful, needy, and anxious to bullying, controlling, and rigid.

- On average, where on this emotional balance spectrum do you see yourself?
- What would you identify as your predominant first-chakra emotion?
- On what behavior pattern or physical manifestation do you base your determination?

D: Yourself and Others

People in your life—perhaps several people—have had a powerful influence on your experience of fundamental safety and your sense of the right to be embodied and exist on this planet. This might be a parent, grandparent, an older sibling, a more distant relative, or a friend or teacher.

- Who in your family had first-chakra issues that you have recognized?
- How did the first-chakra issue manifest in the life of this person (or these persons)?
- What effect did this person (these persons) have on you?
- Who are the people with whom you feel you can live out of your first chakra?
- Who are the people with whom you feel it is not safe for you to live out of the first chakra?

E: Finding Your Authentic Self

- What sort of relationships do you recognize you need in order to better live from your first chakra? (Refer to chapter 4, page 36, if you need to review the kinds of relationships that promote soul growth.)
- How do you express or seek first-chakra energy in your life now?

SECOND-CHAKRA FAMILY KARMA: KAREN'S SEXUAL FANTASIES

Karen is a physician in her 40s who presented for therapy with fantasies of wanting to get erotically involved with a peer at work, although, fortunately, she never acted on them. Karen is a loyal individual who was deeply devoted to her husband, her children, and her patients. Her sexual fantasies were totally incomprehensible to her; they distressed her greatly; keen to understand and prevent acting on them, she sought therapy. My tentative diagnosis was that perhaps she experienced hypomanic episodes, since these few rare instances of sexual fantasies were associated with euphoric mood, less need for sleep, hyperactivity at work, and initiating many new projects.

My initial clinical approach included the usual and customary psychiatric management: initially, we ruled out any medical problem such as a thyroid disorder, kept records on an anti-manic medication and provided her supportive therapy. However, Karen and I both intuitively felt that something was missing in our understanding of her fantasies, and that deeper investigation of the problem was necessary. We dug into her history to get more answers to the puzzling images and questions in her life.

Analytic investigation revealed some startling facts. Karen was an adopted child. Her birth mother was a teenager who had gotten pregnant after relationships with several boys. When her birth mother contacted the likely father, then in the Marines, he offered to help financially but refused to assume paternity as he was unsure if he indeed was the father. Later, her birth mother had made several unsuccessful attempts to abort her. When Karen's birth mother's parents found out, they shipped her away to her uncle and aunt's home in a distant city, and when little Karen was born, they placed her in an orphanage for a few months prior to her adoptive parents taking her.

In her early 40s, Karen learned of her adoption after her adoptive father's death, and driven by some inner force, she set out to search for her biological parents. She traced her mother to another city. Mother was now married to a very stoic and conservative man. She refused to acknowledge or embrace Karen, lest it upset the apple cart of her precariously balanced marriage. Karen contacted her probable biological father, who was cordial but emotionally distant. Crushed, Karen withdrew to her routine life, feeling orphaned all over again.

Feeling hurt, abandoned, unloved, she rededicated herself to her work and her family, but the inner wound festered, driving her to continue scanning her emotional landscape for loving parents. Since they were not forthcoming in her outer life, she internalized them in her soul. In moments of despair, she became her mother. In her fantasy life, she started living and acting out her birth mother who was unavailable in Karen's outer life. Karen's sexual images were a bridge, a way of joining her mother as well as connecting her with an inner parent. To give up these fantasies was to give up her long-lost mother, found and lost soon again.

From a chakra perspective, Karen was caught in the disturbance in her second chakra, which has to do with creating a sense of self by experiencing and acting on instincts. Because of her overactive receptive channel, she became a martyr in her life and work, and fell prey in her fantasies to exploitative men (whose active channel in the second chakra was over-energized). What she was really seeking was the love of and attachment to her parents. Her—and her birth mother's—way to effecting this attachment was via sexual involvement and self-negation. The only way she felt she could secure love, attachment, and parenting from others was by permitting them to exploit her.

We wondered in therapy if Karen's mother might have been the victim of a similar dynamic. Mother was raised in a chaotic family and might have used her sexuality to secure crumbs of attachment. Karen became painfully aware of her biological mother's plight. With insight, empathy, and awareness, she forgave her mother. She also forgave herself for her fantasies. Gradually she became able to be a better parent to herself than her mother had been. Her self-esteem soared. She was blessed with a loving and devoted husband who understood her dynamic and supported her climb out of the deep abyss of her sexual fantasies to reclaim her generative potential and personal authority. Now Karen has deepened her marriage and has risen to a leadership position in her profession and in service to her community. She parents her children, herself, her patients, and her community. Through her suffering and healing, she has retired the family karma inherited from her mother. Like a shaman, she took on her mother's karma, lived it out in fantasy, understood it, overcame it, and reclaimed her dharma, her soul's calling.

Individuals' problems with sexuality or sexual fantasies, especially those of young women and men, are second-chakra issues. What looks like the pursuit of pleasure is really the search for attachment and love from emotionally unavailable parents. Parents who, for whatever reason, cannot bond with and nurture their children impose a karmic burden on them. As teenagers, they may then unconsciously turn to sexuality as a route to relatedness and attachment. This route then creates its own karmic consequences for the teenagers, their parents, the society, and their future children. The vicious cycle continues until someone in the karmic chain interrupts the cycle and restores the dharmic order through suffering, insight, sacrifice, and transformation.

Characteristics of the Second Chakra

The second chakra is situated in the bladder region above the genitals. Its mandala is a six-petalled lotus containing a white circle, symbolizing water, and its totem animal is the crocodile. The second chakra guides the human pursuit of pleasure, attachment, and the sense of being an embodied self. Its developmental goal is generativity, the shadow of which is stagnation of the creative aspects of personality. Its overly-strong assertive channel is characterized by the role of the exploiter while the unbalanced receptive channel manifests in the martyr. When these assertive and receptive energies are balanced in the central channel, the capacity to parent oneself and others emerges. With an unbalanced assertive channel of the second chakra, an individual feels a sense of entitlement. With an unbalanced receptive channel of the second chakra, the individual may experience guilt and anger, but mostly shame.

Brute survival is the issue in the root chakra. When undeveloped, and our energy is active primarily in the second chakra, "the whole aim of life is in sex. Not only is every thought and act sexually motivated, either as a means toward sexual ends or as a compensating sublimation of frustrated sexual zeal, but everything seen and heard is interpreted compulsively, both consciously and unconsciously, as symbolic of sexual themes."[11] Sexual expression does indeed give us a sense of self, but physical sexuality is the primal level of sense of self. When we develop the second chakra, we discover that generativity ranges from genital sexual to all forms of creative expression, not only in art, music, and literature, but in all areas of life. Caroline Shola Arewa writes, "It is through working with this chakra that we come to know our individual beauty, creativity and wisdom. We learn that we belong in the world and that we are welcome here."[12]

Disturbance in the second chakra may manifest medically as genito-urinary system problems and psychiatrically as promiscuity, impotence, low level of self-love, and exploitative and antisocial personality problems.

Journal Exercise: Your Second Chakra

This is the second of seven chakra exercises. As before, this exercise has several parts. Refer to Table 2 as necessary to review the characteristics of the second chakra.

A: Main Function and Developmental Task

The question posed by the first chakra was brute survival, safety, and embodiment. The second chakra has to do with your sense of self: how comfortable and balanced you are with your instinctual energies, as well as your sense of individual beauty, creativity, and wisdom.

- How do you really feel about your instincts?
- How satisfying is your sexual life?
- In what areas of life do you feel creative and generative?
- What sort of "mind talk" do you hear that comments on your instincts and your sense of self?
- Where would you like to be more creative?
- What do other people say about your sexual expression and your creativity?

B: Role Balance

Second chakra roles extend from martyr through self-accepting sovereign to exploiter. As martyr, you submit to others who dominate you. As exploiter, your instinctual impulses dominate and exploit others. When you have achieved role balance, you can receive as well as give, respond as well as initiate.

- What are the situations in which you feel you can accept your sexuality, sensuality, and creativity?
- In what situations do you not feel safe with your sexuality, sensuality, and creativity?

- On a scale from sexual martyr to exploiter, where would you place yourself in general?

C: Emotional State and Balance

When you have achieved a balance, you can experience all your instincts—sexuality, sensuality, creativity, joy in self-expression—feeling safe and at home in your body.

- What are your typical emotions when you think about or engage in sexual, sensual, or creative expression?
- In regard to sexuality, where would you place yourself on the scale from fearful and needy to bullying and controlling?
- What are the areas of life where you would like to feel more comfortable and accepting of your instincts and your creativity?

D: Yourself and Others

Focus now on another person—a member of your family, a friend, or lover—who has had a powerful influence on your self-acceptance.

- How did the second-chakra issues manifest in this person's life? That is, did this individual model as a victim or aggressor in their relationships?
- How did the second-chakra issue manifest in your relationship with this person?
- What effect did this have on you? Do you take on a victim or an aggressor role in significant relationships?

E: Finding Your Authentic Self

- How do you express or seek second-chakra energy in your life now? Do you stifle your sexuality and/or sensuality?
- Do you stifle your creative drive?
- Identify and write down as many ways as you can imagine in which you might express yourself in your sexual and creative sectors differently.
- How is this new approach likely to impact your relationships?
- How are these new choices likely to influence your creative self-expression?

THIRD-CHAKRA FAMILY KARMA:
EDWARD, THE BENEVOLENT TYRANT

Edward is the epitome of an individual stuck in the third chakra as a consequence of his family karma. He is a successful businessman in his late 40s who came for therapy with a diagnosis of manic depression, relationship problems in his marriage, and suffering grief and anger over being pushed out of the family business.

Initially, Edward was emotionally crushed and narcissistically wounded. His dreams indicated the activation of the myth of Icarus. As he rose higher in the corporate ladder, he felt as though he got too close to the sun and his wings melted. He then fell into the ocean where he felt like he was drowning. He experienced these ups and downs as euphoria, depression, and despair.

In therapy, he explored his emotional wounds. Gradually it emerged that he was secretly glad to have been ousted from a burdensome leadership position as CEO of the family business. He exercised his bail-out option and got a reasonable settlement. He secured his basic finances, undertook analysis to get a deeper understanding of his problems and to chart a course for the future in sync with the calling of his soul.

During his analysis, Edward learned how his ambitious paternal grandfather, a stoic German immigrant, established the family business. Grandfather ruled with an iron fist and built his empire one deal at a time. It was assumed that Edward's father would continue in the business, and later the grandsons would follow. When Edward started in the family business, Grandfather was still the power behind the throne. Any attempts Edward made to introduce changes to modernize the company or make it more humane for employees was met with Grandfather's stiff resistance and disapproval. The relationship became so tense that Grandfather did not speak to Edward for several years before his death, except at the contentious board meetings.

After Grandfather's death and Father's retirement, Edward took over the business and it blossomed further. He instituted many changes that modernized the operation and made it more responsive to the needs of his numerous employees. However, although the significantly improved employee morale, loyalty, and participation made the business more humane, Edward's innovations minimally altered the bottom line. The marginal short-term impact on profits became the focus of a corporate war between Edward and his more ambitious brother who eventually ousted him from the corporation by having Edward demoted to middle management.

Edward's childhood memories were of a father who was emotionally unavailable and a mother who was a depressed, "corporate wife" and unable to nurture him. Edward became a tough young man who made his mark on the business soon after he returned from the Vietnam War. He identified with his father and grandfather, becoming a benevolent tyrant at work and in his marriage. He was the indisputable master who relegated his wife and employees to the status of emotional slaves. In his childhood, he had felt enslaved to the burning ambitions of his father and grandfather, and now he projected this inner slave feeling onto the people closest to him.

But after loosing the corporate war, Edward himself felt like a prisoner of war, once again a slave. On this occasion, he did not compensate for this feeling by re-establishing the master persona. Rather, in analysis, he was able to explore his history and recognize how he had been carrying the karma of his grandfather's ambitions. Deep inside, Edward was a caring, soulful man, potentially attentive to his inner life, attached to his wife and children, keen to make a humane impact on his community.

It became clear that getting caught in his grandfather's ambition got him stuck in his third chakra, the seat of self-assertion and personal power. Clinically, his third chakra problem manifested as manic episodes. Burning ambition and a controlling personality were not his authentic nature, but a residue of his grandfather's personality in him that he had felt obliged to perpetuate. Relationally, he would enact his grandfather's master role, enslaving those closest to him.

Whenever insight or circumstances pushed him out of his third chakra, such as when he was forced out of his company, he was psychologically in a "no man's land" that felt like a void. When depressed, he was more soulful, better connected to his wife, children, and peers. In time, he started to understand and honor his feelings (the realm of the fourth or heart chakra). He realized that feelings and relationships were more important to him than control or power over others. When he looked at his world, himself, and his relationships from his grandfather's eyes, he experienced the feeling part of himself as weak and meek. He confused this with depression. Then he felt like Icarus who had lost his wings, about to drown in the dark ocean of emotions beneath him.

As Edward claimed his authentic nature in the realm of the heart (fourth) chakra, he was able to reconfigure his third chakra exercise of personal power and control. Instead of being ensnared in the master-slave dynamic, he could establish genuine partnership with his wife. Together they started a cabinet-making business, something he had always wanted to do. In his spare time, he volunteered for Big Brothers, mentoring young men in distress. We speculated that perhaps this was the sublimation of his wish to mentor and guide his ambitious younger brother (who had pushed him out of the family business), to lead him into the mysteries of the soul's calling, and rescue him from the burdensome karma created by their grandfather.

Characteristics of the Third Chakra

The third chakra is located just above the naval, in the area of the solar plexus. The symbol of the third chakra is an inverted triangle, surrounded by a circle with ten petals on its circumference. Its emblem or symbol is fire. Psychologically, the third chakra is concerned with self-assertion and effectiveness: the exercise of personal power and the expression of enthusiasm. As Joseph Campbell aptly characterizes it, "Here the energy turns to violence and its aim is to consume, to master, to turn the world into oneself and one's own. . . . for now even sex becomes an occasion, not of erotic experience, but of achievement,

conquest, self-assurance, and frequently, also, of revenge."[13] On a physical level, the third chakra relates to all the digestive organs: stomach,
small intestine, liver, gallbladder, and spleen.

When your third chakra is balanced, you feel an abundance of
inner wealth that moves you successfully toward the higher chakras.
Nothing holds you back. You trust your emotions as sources of information, but they do not rule you. You can experience rage when
abused, but you don't have to inflict it on others because you know
your warrior nature. But with either too much or too little "fire in the
belly"—the typical experience of the third chakra—you go to excess or
become immobilized. You are unfeeling and uncaring; fearful and mis-
trusting; or quick-tempered; controlled by anger; violent; loud and
aggressive; prone to acting before thinking. Medically, disturbances in
the third chakra manifest as all types of digestive problems, fatigue and
low energy, eating disorders, headaches and eye problems.

By its very nature, the third chakra is the place where conflicts
arise. You struggle emotionally with opposites: your head and your gut
battle it out. Self-development is most difficult in the third chakra
because our whole society has difficulties dealing with emotions and
power.

In clinical practice, we have encountered numerous outwardly successful men and women who are caught in the assertive channel of their
third (power) chakra. They are hard-driving, competitive, "Type-A"
individuals who build corporate empires but often leave the carnage of
broken relationships and wounded others in their quest. They thus create a burden of karma.

On closer inspection of their life stories in therapy, we are amazed
to learn how caring, feeling, and gentle some of these individuals are
when they unmask their souls after sustaining some hurt or disappointment. It is as if a failure gives them permission to take off their
armor so that they can then show their gentler, kinder side.

More often than not, the power drive and the consequent entrapment in the third chakra is the unresolved karma of their family which

they assume and carry unquestioningly until some profound disappointment stops them in their tracks and forces them to reassess the imbalance in the equation of their life. Then they undertake soul work and reclaim their more authentic calling. Often this involves discovering their fourth (or a higher) chakra. They then become attentive to their relationships via the fourth chakra, or become the spokespersons for the underdog via their fifth chakra, or assume leadership in their community under the auspices of their sixth chakra of leadership, or become mentors and guides to their protégés to honor their seventh chakra.

Journal Exercise: Your Third Chakra

By now you are probably used to chakra journal exercises. As before, open your journal to blank, facing pages. Refer to the chakra table (Table 2 on pages 60–61) as necessary. For the third chakra, consider the following:

A: Main Function and Developmental Task
The main function and task of the third chakra is personal power, initiative, and enthusiasm, the "fire in the belly."

- What do you really believe about your personal initiative and power?
- What sort of "mind talk" about your initiative and power do you hear that you may not actually say aloud?
- What do other people say that supports or contradicts your opinion of yourself and your mind talk?

B: Role Balance
Developing appropriate self-assertion, initiative, and personal effectiveness, and experiencing enthusiasm and passion in your various life roles is the challenge of the third chakra.

- How satisfied are you with your effectiveness and with your ability to assert yourself?
- How effective and powerful do you feel in your relationships?
- How effective and powerful do you feel in your job or profession?

- On the scale from drudge/slave to tyrant/dictator, where would you place yourself?
- How self-assertive and effective do you feel in other areas of your life?
- Where would you like to take more initiative, and be more powerful, assertive, and effective?
- What do other people say about your sense of enterprise?

C: Emotional State and Balance

Third-chakra emotions can be pretty "hot": joy or disgust; delight or despair; and more. The challenge is to be able to experience all emotions, understand that they provide information you need, but not be controlled by them.

- What are your typical emotions when you think about taking initiative or asserting yourself?
- What is your relationship between your "gut and head?"
- What emotions typically rule you?
- What emotions do you typically feel comfortable with?
- What emotions do you typically override?

D: You and Others

Now is a good time to work through this third-chakra exercise focusing on someone in your life who has had a powerful influence on you. This might be a parent, grandparent, an older sibling, a more distant relative, or a friend or teacher.

- How does/did the issue of power, initiative, and enthusiasm manifest with this person?
- What effect does/did this relationship have on you emotionally?
- What role do/did you assume with this person?

E: Finding Your Authentic Self

Now you have identified a significant person who has impacted your capacity to experience and express your personal power, initiative and enthusiasm.

- How might you remedy any deficiencies or excesses you have recognized?
- How can you integrate these changes into other areas of your life?

FOURTH-CHAKRA FAMILY KARMA:
SEX WITH THE STEPSON

Paul, a therapist, is a man in his 50's who consulted us because he was distressed by his sexual relationship with his 14-year-old stepson. Paul was repentant and depressed; and, although the behavior had stopped, he wanted to understand the underlying dynamics lest he be tempted again to act out with another teenage boy.

Paul himself had had a stepfather, George, who married Paul's mother when Paul was in his early teens. George had engaged Paul in sexually inappropriate behavior from early on, and Paul had not been able to end it because he felt torn: if he put a stop to it, he believed, his stepfather would leave him and his mother. And so in order to prevent the stepfather abandoning them, Paul had endured George's advances even though he found them highly unpleasant. The sexual relationship continued for several years until at one point Paul and George had a big blow up about Paul's schooling. Unfortunately, Paul and his stepfather were never able to discuss what soured their relationship, which had begun with warmth and legitimate affection on both sides. Paul had a fourth chakra problem, as did his stepfather.

When George was in his middle teens, his father had abandoned George, his mother, and his siblings. George had supported his mother and his four younger brothers while finishing high school and putting himself through college during the Great Depression of the 1930's. George once told Paul that he had felt terribly lonely and abandoned when his father was no longer there to help him with his math home-work.

George had started a sexual relationship with his stepson, Paul, in an attempt to reconstitute his experience of the father-son relationship, and—since Paul's relationship with his stepfather, George, was unsatisfactory—Paul had engaged in sex with his stepson. Both George and

Paul had dropped from the fourth chakra of love, connection, and heart-level Eros to the second chakra, which is the other chakra where the feeling of connectedness—Eros—is predominant, but on a sexual level. The attempt to enlist the second chakra to satisfy the fourth chakra problem is, of course, doomed to failure and disappointment for all involved.

In therapy with Paul, we understood the dynamic of his fourth chakra frustration: his inability to receive love and caring from his stepfather, and his father hunger. We worked through his regressive attempts to manage this via the second chakra sexual Eros, and he gradually started to make a deeper, authentic loving connection with his wife, who was extremely supportive of his therapeutic efforts while helping him set limits with his stepson.

When men and women can't experience authentic love, intimacy, and caring in the fourth chakra, they often regress to the second chakra, resorting to sexual Eros in their desperate attempt to feel the deep, longed-for connection. In clinical practice this is one of the most frequent problems our patients experience in relationships. Sexual encounters of this kind are archaic, misguided attempts at establishing a heart-to-heart and soul-to-soul relationship. One person submits to the sexual advances to get a sense of affiliation, connection, and relationship; and the other person imposes his or her sexualized need for connection. Two lonely souls reenact the hopeless second-chakra drama of the exploiter and the victim/martyr. Resorting to a sexual liaison does not lead to a truly creative encounter between two people but rather becomes an exploitative situation.

The alliance between the exploiter and the victim/martyr is a form of archaic relationship in which, if the two people are willing to pay the psychological exploitation tax, they get a somewhat primitive sense of fellowship with each other. The crumbs of affiliation manifested in such an encounter feed an inner identification with the exploiter. Because of the inner twinship with the exploiter, the martyr/victim later in life reenacts the drama. Thus men and women who have been sexually exploited as children or young people often reenact the dynamic, becoming exploiters themselves.

But there is another variation of the drama of second and fourth chakra problems. When two souls cannot consummate Eros—when the partnership cannot be a partnership of the mind, body, and soul because of fears of emotional victimization, exploitation, and enslavement—many individuals unfortunately shut themselves totally off from relational possibilities. Such women and men present clinically with multiple relationship failures and difficulty in establishing true, trusting, mutual relationships at the fourth chakra level. As a matter of fact, the higher the level of the individual's integrity, the more he or she would withdraw from all relationships rather than risk reenacting the exploiter-victim drama or acting out the identification with the exploiter. In a sense, they are trying to protect the people they love from the exploiter within.

While there are important social, theoretical, and clinical implications of this drama of second and fourth chakra—of the wish for intimacy at the fourth chakra level being solved regressively by sexual Eros in the second chakra, and the unfortunate sexual acting out inherent in such a regression—this does not root out the cause. Unless this dynamic is understood fundamentally and attended to, the cycle perpetuates at some other level. What a sexual abuser and—just as importantly—the victim are seeking in their collusion is genuine caring, love, and affiliation. But since both participants in the drama have not had mature identifications that foster a truly loving and caring relationship at the fourth chakra level, they do the best they can, which is to regress to the second chakra and play out the wish for love in the realm of sexual Eros.

When society and therapists can bring love and compassion to their understanding of this sort of sexual acting out and abuse while still setting appropriate limits, then, and only then, can the dynamic be healed. Only then will abusers and victims discover a truly caring, fourth chakra where primal drives are transformed into mutual love.

Characteristics of the Fourth Chakra

When we cross the diaphragm from the third to the fourth, also referred to as the heart, chakra, we move from the realm of compulsive instincts and drives to the beginnings of the "new life." The heart chakra "is really the center where psychical things begin, the recognition of values and ideas."[14] Here, we begin to become conscious in a new way. All three lower chakras are modes of our living in the world in our native state, "outward turned: the modes of the lovers, the fighters, the builders, the accomplishers," and our "joys and sorrows on these levels are functions of achievements in the world 'out there,' what people think of one, what has been gained, what lost."[15]

The fourth chakra presides over the developmental task of transforming compulsive instincts (those of the first, second, and third chakra energies) into intimacy. Symbolically it is represented by a hexagonal mandala with twelve petals, and is governed by the element air; its totem animal is the antelope or gazelle

When we are unable to accomplish the developmental task of the fourth chakra, we feel a sense of emotional isolation. In the unbalanced assertive channel, this chakra is experienced as the caretaker mode, and in the receptive channel as the dependent mode. When these assertive and receptive energies are balanced in the fourth chakra, we experience the inner lover; we are capable of giving and receiving. Disturbances in the fourth chakra manifest medically as cardiac problems and psychiatrically as difficulty in expressing feelings, depression, and codependency disorders.

Journal Exercise: Your Fourth Chakra

In many ways, the fourth-chakra challenge is the greatest facing humankind. Greed; rampant, unrelated sexuality; and unchecked, hot-tempered aggression—perverted manifestations of the first, second, and third chakras, respectively—threaten our collective existence as civilized beings. The fourth is the chakra where we make the transition to the beginnings of enlightenment.

A: Main Function and Developmental Task

The task and the opportunity of the fourth, or heart, chakra is to transform the potentially compulsive energies of the "lower" three chakras into relatedness and intimacy.

- What are the situations in which you feel compassion and intimacy free from the compulsive energies of the first three chakras?
- What experiences do you recall that helped you experience the energy of the fourth chakra?

B: Role Balance

Fourth chakra roles range from the co-dependent end, where you can be a caretaker or devourer, through the balanced expression of the heart chakra energy as a compassionate, selfless lover, to the other extreme where you go through the motions of "loving" but really are only performing, acting as though you are relating from the heart.

- Make a list of the people to whom you feel emotionally close. Then characterize the sort of role you assume with each one: Are you more caretaker/devourer, selfless lover, or performer?

C: Emotional State and Balance

When your fourth chakra is balanced in its expression, you can experience compassion and selfless love. The unbalanced state ranges from isolation to co-dependency.

- What are your typical emotions when you think about or engage in a significant relationship?
- Look at the list of people you made in section B of this exercise. What sort of emotion do you experience with each one? Do you feel isolated? Co-dependent? Or connected, compassionate, but also free to be yourself?
- In what relationship would you like to establish a deeper sense of emotional connectedness?
- What do other people say about your capacity to be loving and compassionate?

D: You and Others

Focus now on a member of your family who has had a powerful influence on you. This might be a parent, a grandparent, an older sibling, or a more distant relative.

- How did the fourth-chakra issues manifest in the life of this person? That is, did this individual model as loving, caring, and emotionally present, or disengaged and distant?
- How did the fourth-chakra issue manifest in your relationship with this person?
- What effect did this have on you? Do you take on a caretaker or dependent role in relationships?
- Generally, how has your family experience affected your fourth-chakra balance?

E: Finding Your Authentic Self

Now that you have identified a significant family member who has modeled a caretaker, dependent, or mutual role in their relationships, let us explore how you might modify your choices.

- Identify and write down as many ways as you can imagine in which you might take on a different role with the significant persons you have identified. For example, if you have been in the caretaker role, what would it feel like to try out the dependent or mutual role?
- How do you imagine these modified approaches are likely to impact your relationships?
- How are these new choices likely to influence your sense of emotional connectedness and mutuality?

FIFTH-CHAKRA FAMILY KARMA:
ANN FINDS HER VOICE

Ann came for psychoanalysis after attending my (Ashok Bedi's) lecture at the local psychiatric hospital community education program on the subject of spirituality and healing. I noted intuitively that her choice to consult me after hearing my voice was perhaps related to her search for her own voice, which she might have projected onto my voice. In due course, my intuition bore out as somewhat relevant.

Ann is a therapist in her late 40s. She was born to a Jewish family in New York City. Her grandparents on both sides of her family had fled the Nazi terror in Europe. Several aunts had perished in Hitler's concentration camps. When Ann's family moved to California during her middle-school years, Ann discovered she was one of only a few Jewish students in large school. Her parents quickly assimilated in the gentile culture, underplaying their Jewish roots, lest it provoke any turbulence.

Ann was the oldest of several brothers and sisters. Her father was an upwardly-mobile professional, while mother was a depressed housewife. Both parents were emotionally unavailable. Ann became the caretaker of her mother and younger siblings. As she got embedded in her caretaker complex, she became less and less able to express her needs and views. At her large school, she felt marginalized as a "closet Jew," clumped with a few other Jewish peers. In her late teens she got pregnant and soon married the father of her child, thereby manifesting her unconscious wish to escape the caretaker burden and cultural entrapment she felt in her milieu. This may have gotten her away from her family, but not out of her caretaker role. Her first marriage lasted only a short time, and she remarried soon after.

Both of her marriages were ostensibly to powerful men who, unfortunately, projected their dependency onto her and really needed Ann to take care of them. Once again, she was trapped in her caretaker complex. She perceived her two husbands as loud intimidators, incapable of authentic communication and intimacy, and her own voice in these relationships was once again muffled. Cut off from her family's Jewish roots, Ann knew no means to communicate with Spirit. Her soul silenced, her voice enfeebled, her needs trivialized, she finally sought therapy to rediscover her own voice.

In therapy, she retraced her family's history. Nazi death camps had silenced her ancestors' voices; the gentile mainstream inundated her Jewish spirit; her parents' struggle for integration into the American melting pot had overwhelmed her developmental needs; her two dominating, needy husbands' loud demands had subjugated her personal needs. Her mute soul was screaming for acknowledgement and affirmation.

Slowly but surely, Ann confronted her persona of the silent sufferer. Even in therapy sessions, she would speak initially in a timid, hushed tone. Gradually, as she found her voice, her expression became more robust, her soul more empowered, her spirit took wing as she rediscovered her spiritual source. She started speaking up. After several months' therapy, she developed into a formidable public speaker who could advocate for her patients and herself. She came out of the closet as a Jew and joined the local temple where a woman Rabbi took her under her wings and groomed her for a leadership position in the congregation. While her own mother was unavailable, her soul arranged for an emotionally corrective experience by finding her the Rabbi, teacher, and godmother. Life and soul has a mysterious way of concluding the unfinished chapters of our life, if we follow the contours of our destiny.

Ann's problem—being a member of a disenfranchised community—is also the problem of women throughout the world. Minority men in the West, immigrants, and the citizens of the third world face similar fifth-chakra problems. They become silent sufferers, their voices muffled and souls censured by the more powerful and politically enfranchised. When the underdogs cannot express their own voice, they regress to the dynamic of the first chakra. They become aggressors; they may resort to gang affiliations, political movements, and terrorist activities to claim their own ground. The dynamics of the first through the fifth chakras are intrinsically interwoven. It is important for politicians, psychologists and policy makers to be aware of this dynamic if they wish to attend to these problems in a humane and equitable manner.

Characteristics of the Fifth Chakra

The fifth chakra is located in the throat area. Symbolically, a circle with sixteen petals represents its mandala. Its totem animal is a white elephant and its element ether (commonly understood as "spirit," *prana*, or *chi*). The fifth chakra regulates the developmental tasks of initiative, "the power of the word."

Having gotten a glimpse of Higher Spirit in the heart chakra, "the whole desire of the heart [in the fifth chakra] will be to learn to know it more fully, to hear it, not through things and within during certain fortunate moments only, but immediately and forever."[16] Sound and hearing from all planes of existence come together in this, the throat chakra.

Blockages of the throat chakra result in a limited awareness, lack of creativity, and sense of isolation in the universe, causing deep grief and longing. People often turn to various sorts of external activities to fill the inner void created by their alienation from Spirit.

The unbalanced assertive channel of the throat chakra manifests as the rude, bombastic, loud-mouthed, self-righteous intimidator while the unbalanced receptive channel expresses as loneliness, isolation, and a sense of meaninglessness. When the assertive and receptive energies are balanced in the central channel, the articulate communicator and leader, who is able to sense and attune to energy and to maintain a disciplined spiritual practice, emerges. Medically, fifth-chakra disturbances manifest as throat and thyroid problems; exhaustion or hyperactivity; ear, nose, and throat disorders; weight gain/loss problems. Emotional conditions are anxiety disorders, and character and narcissistic personality disorders.

Journal Exercise: Your Fifth Chakra

A: Main Function and Developmental Task
Communication at all levels of Being is the main function of the fifth chakra, and opening to Spirit is the developmental task.

- What are the areas in your life in which you are comfortable saying what you think and feel?
- How well do you sense and attune to energy?
- What energies in other people do you experience most often? Their pain? Their anxiety? Their joy?
- As you look back over your life, what are the stages you have gone through in your sensitivity to and communication with Spirit?

B: Role Balance

Your capacity to effectively express yourself as well as listen at many levels is the challenge of the fifth chakra. When assertive and receptive channels are balanced, you experience peacefulness, harmony, and stillness.

- How authentic and confident do you feel in expressing your viewpoint?
- In what situations do you feel able to communicate your views and where do you feel thwarted in freedom to express yourself?
- On a scale from inhibited to effective communicator and listener to intimidator/demagogue, where would you place yourself?
- What do other people say about your capacity to communicate your views, values, thoughts, feelings, and spiritual insights?

C: Emotional State and Balance

When we are aware of and can communicate with Spirit, we experience peacefulness, stillness, and harmony. For most of us, this degree of balance is an ideal close to sainthood. More often, our experience ranges from feeling insensitive, dull, cut off through moments or periods of harmony and peacefulness, on to feeling self-righteous, tactless, and verbose.

- What are your typical emotions when you think about expressing your true thoughts and feelings?
- Make a list of thoughts, feelings, and beliefs that you can express authentically.
- Make a list of thoughts, feelings, and beliefs that you inauthentically express.

D: You and Others

Work through this exercise focusing on a member of your family who has had a powerful influence on you. This might be a parent, a grandparent, an older sibling, or a more distant relative.

• Regarding your relationships, where would you place yourself on the scale from dull and inhibited through effective communicator to authentic and spiritually grounded?
• How did the fifth-chakra issues manifest in your family?
• What effect did this have on you? Do you tend to communicate authentically or inhibit your true thoughts and feelings?

E: Finding Your Authentic Self

Now that you have identified a significant family member who has modeled fifth-chakra expression, let us explore how you might modify your choices.

• Identify and write down as many ways as you can imagine in which you might express or inhibit your true voice.
• How might modifying your usual fifth-chakra style to be more authentic impact your life and relationships?
• How are these new choices likely to influence your sense of yourself?

SIXTH-CHAKRA FAMILY KARMA: RUTH EMERGES AS A LEADER

Ruth comes from a family of powerful men. Her grandfather was a successful entrepreneur who built a major company and left Ruth and her siblings a large estate and trust fund. However, he also left a very dark legacy: He sodomized Ruth from age six through twelve. Ruth has worked several decades to detoxify this shadow legacy of her grandfather's karma.

Ruth is a soulful woman who married a powerful man—a spiritual leader in public but in private just as emotionally abusive as her grandfather. After three decades of unhappy marriage, her husband ran off with a younger woman. Depleted and drained, Ruth sought therapy, first with one therapist, then with another, and eventually with a third. She was a follower looking for a leader, a healer to soothe and restore her soul. She felt that two of her previous therapists abandoned her when they rather precipitously relocated to another state.

In her analysis, Ruth projected onto her therapist her wish for a leader and a healer/guide. Her fantasy was that if she were a good enough follower, a compliant patient, somehow she would be healed. Embedded in her leader/follower transference was the reenactment of the pattern with her abusive grandfather. Unconsciously, she felt that if only she were a good little girl, she could transform her grandfather's abuse into love. Her wish, however, did not materialize as both her marriage and successive therapeutic relationships ended in disappointments.

At first, Ruth experienced any intervention not as psychotherapy but as "psycho-the-rapist." Gradually, together we understood the deep wounds in her psyche. Instead of projecting her inner leader onto the powerful men in her life, and later onto her analyst, she started honoring the leader within. She gradually became the advocate and champion of abused women. This was her soul's calling. Because of her experience of sexual abuse, she was exquisitely sensitive and empathetic to the plight of abused women.

Ruth's trauma had groomed her to be a leader, healer, and champion of abused women. She felt empowered as she gained insight into her dynamic and the meaning of misery in her life story. As she balanced her assertive (leadership) channel and receptive (follower) channel in her sixth chakra, she integrated these energies in her central channel. Now she participates in the lives of abused women, not as their leader but rather as a fellow sufferer in their healing. Her patients are empowered to assume leadership and authority over their own destiny.

People who are abused and traumatized do not need leaders to tell them what to do. They need soul guides, mentors, who can participate in their journey and rekindle their own potential for self-empowerment to take leadership in their lives. Like Ruth, abused individuals often experience the psychotherapist as "psycho-the-rapist." Frequently this reputation is justified when therapists either sexually or emotionally abuse their clients in a karmic repetition cycle. Emotionally needy individuals may be attracted to the healing profession, vicariously seeking nurturance by projecting their need for nurturance onto their patients. This perpetuates the cycle of abuse. Ruth had to re-experience this in her marriage and the abandonment in her two previous therapies before we together understood the dark legacy of her grandfather's family karma that she had to re-experience and retire.

Characteristics of the Sixth Chakra

The sixth chakra—sometimes called the "soul-eye"—is located slightly above and between the eyebrows. It regulates the developmental task of establishing inner wisdom, vision, and mastery. Individual mind and intelligence are the psychological aspects of the sixth chakra, and spiritual practices focused on this chakra are intended to raise the level of conscious awareness of the Spirit.

The great 19th-century Indian seer, Sri Ramakrisha (1836–1886), taught that when God-consciousness falls short, traditions become dogmatic and oppressive, and religious teachings lose their transforming power.[17] Of the sixth chakra he said:

> When the mind reaches this plane, one witnesses divine revelations day and night. Yet even then there remains a slight consciousness of "I." Having seen the unique manifestation man becomes mad with joy as it were and wishes to be one with the all-pervading Divine, but cannot do so. It is like the light of a lamp inside a glass case. One feels as if one could touch the light, but the glass intervenes and prevents it.[18]

Work on the sixth chakra "is of utmost importance," Caroline Shola Arewa writes, "because it is through extending our perception that . . . we learn to see beyond the illusion and limitations of ordinary reality."[19] It is through the sixth chakra that the Spirit informs our consciousness of our soul's calling.

The balanced sixth chakra makes possible the experiences of spontaneous spiritual awakening, profound insights, meaning, and clarity in your life, and inner mastery. When the sixth chakra's assertive channel is unbalanced, an individual may become a dictatorial leader, megalomaniac, or abuser of higher powers. And when the receptive channel is unbalanced, a person can become an unquestioning follower or mental slave, imprisoned by lower energies and dismissive of his or her own spiritual experience. Medically, disturbances of the sixth chakra are experienced as headaches and migraines, and psychiatrically as existential depression and lack of meaning in life in spite of outer success.

Journal Exercise: Your Sixth Chakra

A: Main Function and Developmental Task

The center of inner vision resides in the sixth chakra. Hence, the developmental task is to cultivate our clear receptivity to the Divine through the practice of spiritual disciplines that lead to wisdom and subtle perception.

- What sort of spiritual disciplines do you practice? (For example, prayer, meditation, yoga, martial arts, fasting.)
- Which spiritual disciplines have you found most effective in cultivating your receptivity to the Divine?
- If you were to undertake a new spiritual discipline, which one(s) would most appeal to you?

B: Role Balance

The sixth chakra roles range from mental slave and unquestioning follower through the balance seen in the spiritually wise person to the dictatorial leader and abuser of higher powers.

- On a scale from unquestioning follower to dictatorial leader, where would you place yourself?
- What do other people say about your capacity for deeper insight and leadership?

C: Emotional State and Balance

- On the emotion scale from cynicism and skepticism through contentment and stillness of mind and body to spiritual inflation, where do you usually place yourself?
- What are the conditions and situations in which you are clear and centered in your sixth chakra?
- What sorts of experiences push you out of your spiritual center into an unbalanced state or into a lower chakra?
- What do you find you need to do to maintain your centeredness in your sixth chakra more of the time?

D: You and Others

- How did or do sixth-chakra issues manifest in your relationship with a friend or a member of your family who has had a powerful influence on you?
- How did or do sixth-chakra issues manifest in this person's life? That is, did this individual model as a wise and concerned leader, a spiritually mature and responsible person, an inflated false guru, or a cynical skeptic?

E: Finding Your Authentic Self

From the sixth-chakra perspective, your authentic self is a person who has developed inner vision, mastery, and wisdom. Psychologically, the sixth chakra informs individual mind and intelligence; but at a spiritually more developed stage, individual consciousness rises to a conscious awareness of Spirit that informs us of our soul's calling.

- What is your sense of your soul's calling? What is the purpose for which you are on the planet?
- What experiences have led you to your sense of your soul's calling?
- As you increasingly live what you have found to be your soul's calling, how has your relationship with other people changed?
- What do you need to do in order to become your authentic self?
- How would these new choices likely influence your sense of leadership?

SEVENTH-CHAKRA FAMILY KARMA:
ESTHER HEARS THE WHISPERS OF THE SACRED

Esther is a schoolteacher in her early 50s who sought therapy a few years ago when her close friend became very concerned about Esther's extreme social withdrawal. Esther would religiously go to work as a schoolteacher, but outside of that she completely withdrew from all social contact. In her therapy, she often sat motionless and refused or was unable to speak. On my recommendation, she started to maintain and bring her personal daily journal to the therapy session and read it aloud, but otherwise spoke little. When I invited her to explore the dreams she had recorded in her journal, she was unable to associate to them. I consulted my mentors on how to deal with this complex case, and with their concurrence, I started to associate to her dreams on her behalf. Although she would refuse to respond to my comments during the session, she would reflect on them in her journal, which she would read aloud in the following session. Gradually and painstakingly, I established a fragile bridge to her inner life.

Esther was raised on a farm in northern Wisconsin by stoic German immigrant parents. Father was a man of few words. At the dinner table, children were to be seen, not heard. Mother was a loving but subservient woman, and Esther saw herself as the protector of her mother and younger siblings, a role deeply engraved in her psyche to this day. After her father forbade her to date a black fellow student while at the local university, she never dated or married. Later in life, she became a teacher and committed her life to teaching and advocacy for her students and her fellow teachers. Her entire life was devoted to committee meetings and organizations to improve school programs and the status of her fellow teachers.

After a few sessions, the managed care company refused to authorize further therapy on the grounds that Esther was a "non-talking patient." They did not see how any work could be done. Perhaps, in a certain outer sense, they were right. However, Esther and I agreed on a sliding-fee. But in spite of financial hardship, Esther insisted on paying my full fee. It took some persuading to get her to agree to lower her payments.

Therapy with Esther has been one of the most sacred experiences of my life. In her presence, I felt I was in the precinct of a goddess, in the temple of the goddess Shakti. Clinically, Esther was stuck in the receptive channel of the seventh chakra. She was a guide to generations of students in her school. Grandparents who had been her students would bring their grandchildren to her class with respect and reverence. She was a true guru and instilled the highest of moral values in her students. The world is a better place because of Esther and individuals like her.

Gradually, I insisted she attend to her needs for socialization and self-care. Over the years of work with Esther, she has developed some new friendships. She has learned to be as good a mentor and guru for herself as she has long been for generations of students. Esther has found ways to be more at home in the world without losing her profound connection to the Spirit.

Characteristics of the Seventh Chakra

The seventh, or crown, chakra is located just above the top of the head, and is the epitome of the neocortex or the new central system, the seat of evolving consciousness, as compared to the autonomic or involuntary nervous system, the site of our vegetative primal existence, which is focused on survival and security. At the level of the seventh chakra, individuals struggle with metapsychological issues that bridge our humanity and spirituality: the highest and most complex questions of the meaning and mystery of human existence and consciousness in the larger scheme of the cosmos. The developmental task of the seventh chakra is to balance the aspects of our materiality with the concerns of our spirituality.

In the unbalanced assertive channel, the seventh chakra is experienced as narcissism and megalomania. In the unbalanced receptive channel, the seventh chakra is experienced as extreme introversion and often autism, complete withdrawal from outer concerns and relation-ships. When we balance these energies in the central channel, we experience the teacher/guru/guide within. When in touch with this inner mentor, we can detach from material concerns and attend to guiding ourselves and our fellow human beings to their highest soul calling. Then we become a bridge between the soul and the Spirit. This is a tall order. Many who are uninitiated into the realm of the psyche may experience this as inflation and regress to becoming false guides who lead their followers astray. Those who can detach from personal gain and ego-inflating motives have the opportunity to leave this world a much better place than they found it. They are the ones who have realized, for example, Jesus' commandment to take up their crosses and follow Him.

The Christian cross signifies many things to many people. From the viewpoint of the seventh chakra, it symbolizes the tension between the soul's spiritual calling and the earth's demands. The horizontal axis is concerned with our material and outer concerns. The vertical axis of the cross symbolizes the calling of our soul and our connection with the Holy Spirit in this lifetime. How we balance these concerns embodies how we bear our cross in this life.

It is the Hindu belief that our soul travels for aeons in the process of maturation until it achieves its highest potential when it becomes purified and free from the cumbersome cycle of reincarnations and achieves *moksha*, or nirvana. At this point of clarity, purification, and maturity, the soul is ready to merge with the Spirit. Thus purified, the water in the earthly vessel is ready to be poured back into the timeless cosmic ocean of the divine Spirit. "If we remove that glasslike barrier of which Ramakrishna spoke, both our God and ourselves will explode then into light, sheer light, one light, beyond names and forms, beyond thought and experience, beyond even the concepts of 'being' and 'non-being.'"[20] Soul and Spirit become one. This is the highest state of con-sciousness. The soul that has thus traveled long and far in time and space is an old soul. Usually the old souls play out the drama of the seventh chakra in this lifetime.

Journal Exercise: Your Seventh Chakra

The journal exercise for the seventh chakra differs from the journal exercises for the other six chakras. Devote a section of your journal to the seventh chakra. The first part is for your personal experiences.

A. Personal Peak Spiritual Experiences

• Take time to recall and write down your peak spiritual experiences, those experiences of selfless oneness.

• What was conducive to your having those peak spiritual experiences?

• So far as you know, what makes it difficult for you to have more peak spiritual experiences?

B: Others' Peak Spiritual Experiences that You Know About

• Whom do you know about who has had peak spiritual experiences? This may be someone you know personally, or a spiritual master, saint, guru, etc.

• As you explore the life of the person or persons who have had peak spiritual experiences, what do you notice about their way of life?

• What do or have these people said or written about their spiritual life?

C: Putting It All Together

• What inferences do you draw from both your experience and the peak spiritual experiences of the people you thought about in the previous part of this exercise?

◆　◆　◆

Each of the seven chakras is the psycho-spiritual focal point of certain attitudes, emotions, behaviors, and physical organ systems. When a chakra's assertive and receptive channels are out of balance, we experience typical spiritual, attitudinal, emotional, and physical symptoms. Some of this imbalance may be the karmic legacy of ancestors—parents, grandparents, etc.—whose corresponding chakras were unbalanced. We, their descendants, inherit the task of righting the imbalance, so that the family's karma does not devolve onto yet another generation. It's up to us whether or not "the buck stops here."

Part Two

WORKING OUT
YOUR FAMILY KARMA

6

CLUES TO KARMA AND
HOW TO SORT THEM OUT

Once, somebody asked Jung what the technique was for dealing with the shadow, that dimension of our personality that we won't or can't see because it relativizes what we believe we are. Jung's answer was on the mark: "If one can speak of technique at all, it consists solely in an attitude. First of all one has to accept and to take seriously into account the existence of the shadow. Secondly, it is necessary to be informed about its qualities and intentions. Thirdly, long and difficult negotiations may well be unavoidable."[1] The same holds true for karma and family karma.

First, you have to realize that something is working on you over which you have little control. This realization demands courage: the courage to question your habitual attitudes and behaviors; the courage to face the unknown; and the courage to risk transformation. What will you encounter? Who will you be if you grapple with that unknown and change in the process?

Second, you have to inform yourself. You have to gain insight. What is the legacy, the karmic inheritance? How does it serve you? How does it constrain you? Whose karma is it that you carry?

Third, you must be ready to negotiate with yourself and with the people close to you. Negotiating with yourself is perhaps the most difficult part, because of the human tendency to believe that we are masters in our own minds and hearts. But of course, we aren't. As we all know, from time to time "something gets into us" over which we have little control, and "we just aren't ourselves" for the time being. A complex gets activated or a transpersonal (or archetypal) force possesses us. Personal and family karma, however, are more like patterns or habits, ways of being, persistent attitudes, whereas when complexes or transpersonal forces are constellated, they behave like intruders, disturbers of the peace. When you start to alter patterns and habits, you may feel unsettled, perhaps afraid, unsure of yourself.

With optimal self-object experiences we discussed in chapter 4, the potential of the self evolves. The maturation of your potential evokes a sense of hope, of a future richer than your past. You begin to sense that your behavior has meaning and purpose to those around you. You can take comfort in knowing that you are in the presence of propitious energies that will incubate and nurture your emerging potential. You come to believe in a benevolent, just order, a supportive milieu, a belief that gradually evolves into one of the highest attributes of the human psyche: a sense of faith in the goodness of yourself and in the surrounding Being.

This sense of faith that blossoms from optimal self-object experiences is the single most important ingredient that will help you transcend the curses of family karma and transmute them into a blessing for yourself and the world. Transmuting your family karma leaves the world a better place for all humanity, and is your contribution to raising human consciousness to a higher plane.

WHERE WE START:
AWARENESS, KNOWLEDGE, RESPONSIBILITY

The prerequisites and foundation for attending to your personal and family karma are awareness of what you experience, knowledge of the ways personal and family karma manifests in your life, and the realization that you are responsible for working to change what does not serve you well. We will consider each of these points individually.

Awareness

Awareness means paying attention to what is happening in you and around you. Some people get lost in the so-called "outer" world, and some get lost in the so-called "inner" world. This distinction is actually somewhat artificial, because we all live in both worlds and they influence each other all the time. So we have to pay attention to both.

We respond or react to what happens around us and in us with some mix of actions and emotions. As we have seen in the stories recounted in earlier chapters, our personal and family complexes, chakra imbalances, relationship patterns, and medical and psychiatric conditions predispose us to perceive, act, and react in ways that may not suit our authentic nature or the situation at hand. Conversely, these same personal and inherited constraints (our inner structure) function as selective filters, as rose-colored or mud-colored glasses, and set us up to perceive and experience what happens around us, to us, and in us according to their emotional coloration.

Awareness is the first step. Nothing will change unless you notice that what is happening "inside" and "outside" does not always work well for you. Knowledge, your second ally, helps you focus your awareness.

Knowledge

Useful knowledge is both concept and content. In the previous chapters, we presented many examples of women and men who are dealing with various manifestations of their personal and family karma.

The component of knowledge refers to the notion of karma as actions and their consequences (the law of cause and effect in human life), and the various ways in which personal and family karma can and does manifest in individuals. Observation provides the necessary content of your knowledge. How you and your parents, grandparents, and other relatives experience things; how you and they act and react; what strongly attracts or repels you and them; what you and they struggle with and what comes easily; where you and they are split and are of "two minds;" where and how you and they chose to work, love, and play; what comes to you in fantasies and dreams—all these and more fill in the conceptual knowledge with living details.

By paying attention and having conceptual and detailed knowledge, you have what you need to deal responsibly and constructively with your karmic legacy.

Responsibility

You can respond to your karma in either of two ways: you can lay blame, or you can shoulder the burden and try to lighten it through your efforts. Blaming really doesn't get you anywhere; it's a waste of time and energy. Indeed, you do often suffer the consequences of other's actions; and whether or not you choose to be born into your present body and circumstances is an unanswerable metaphysical question. Here you are. Now what are you going to do about it?

Blaming is pretty much a conscious choice; the subtler dimension of responsibility is to recognize and withdraw projections of which we are mostly unconscious. In chapter 5, we talked about the unconscious: all those personal memories, feelings, impulses, emotions, and behaviors that you are unaware of when your waking mind is occupied, as well as innate patterns that structure emotion and behavior. Projections happen to you. You confront, in other people, these memories, emotional patterns, etc., that you don't recognize in yourself. Or, more precisely, your unseen face confronts you in other people. Taking responsibility for projections means that you have to recognize what it is about the other person that mirrors something in you that you don't otherwise see. Unpleasant projections happen to us most frequently when something touches one of our feeling-toned complexes and exceeds our capacity to manage the energy within ourselves. You can grow in maturity as you take responsibility for unpleasant projections. But in your projections, you also see what you have not yet become but could develop into. (We discussed these sorts of projections in chapter 4 as relationships that secure, challenge, and befriend your soul.)

TOOLS FOR THE SEARCH

From our discussion so far, you may have deduced that several external and historic sources of information provide crucial data in assessing the karmic debts and gifts of your ancestors. Some of the sources of information include a family history, family albums, and family myths and stories you may hear from a distant uncle or aunt. Often these myths and stories, discussed only in hushed tones at the outer edges of family get-togethers by marginalized family members, can be a very rich source of information about clan karma.

For instance, it is common in our practice for our patients to report rumors about abuse or family shame that are not discussed in the mainstream family events. When our patients get this information, it suddenly makes sense to them why they have intimacy fears, trust issues, or relationship problems. They are eclipsed by the dark shadow of ancestral karma that gets activated whenever they try to get close to another person. Often they have similar difficulties in establishing trust with a therapist for fear of being exploited and abused.

Journal Exercise: Family Legends and Rumors

In your journal, dedicate a section to reporting the following:

- Stories that are commonly repeated about your parents or grandparents.
- Rumors you may have heard regarding family members, and who reported the rumor to you. If there are variations on the story, note what these are and who told them. How are these people related to the subject of the story?
- What are the stories you hear other family members tell about you? Are they related to another family member's story? How do you feel about it?
- Can you see a possible effect of the story in your or another family member's life?

Search for Your Roots

What each one of us does as an individual, we do as a group, as nations and cultures. For instance, the roots of American culture bear the karmic legacy of patricide (severance of the authority of the British Empire), rugged individualism with emphasis on individual rights over collective well-being, and our national shadow: extermination of the first inhabitants of this continent, the Native American peoples, and the enslavement of our African-American brothers and sisters. Unless we understand and assimilate the light and shadow of our national roots, we will continue to act out this collective shadow. To this day, we continue to be besieged by the national shadow in the form of our racial problems, difficulty in providing health care for the poor and vulnerable sectors of our communities, and the highest infant mortality rate in the Western world in this richest and strongest nation on Earth.

The distillate of all the cumulative karma of human ancestors, beginning with our primal parents, Adam and Eve, is contained in the unique structures called archetypes. They embody the light and the dark of collective wisdom and villainy. For instance, under the auspices of the archetype of the Great Mother, we may learn to trust the caring embrace of humanity and all its gifts. Yet, the same archetype can be experienced as the Terrible Devouring Mother, usurping our potential for independence, autonomy, and self-assertion in deference to a child-like dependence on mother figures or maternal institutions, such as groups, movements, or fanatical fundamentalist religious sects. In our clinical work, we have found that it is crucial to identify what archetypes are activated in our lives and the lives of our patients, and whether they befriend or befuddle us or them on the path to the soul.

Journal Exercise: Where Are Your Roots?

If you don't know your family background, take some time to find out where your maternal and paternal families came from. You might start by interviewing family members. Perhaps one of them has an old family Bible with birth, marriage, and death records. (To help you with this search, there is a detailed resources guide in Appendix B.)

- What were the special challenges that your families of origin had to face as a result of their ethnic, religious, or national origin?
- What can you identify as your family of origin's ethnic, religious, or national karma?
- What can you identify as your family of origin's special talents?
- How are these manifest in your life today?

FAMILY KARMA AND ADOPTED CHILDREN

The controversy between nature and nurture runs deep in psychology and the understanding of the human psyche. Nowhere else is this issue highlighted more than in the issue of adopted children. Would their psyches conform to nature and biological determinism, or would it be patterned by environmental imprinting? One of the key questions in family karma is whether it is the result of family milieu and family dynamics in which the growing child is caught and thus turned into the container for a certain part of family dysfunction, or whether the family karma is transmitted exclusive of the immediate family dysfunction, that is, not by learning or imitation. We are proposing that family karma is also transmitted through unconscious means, transgenerationally, via archetypal mechanisms rather than by direct learning from family members' behavior and example.

In our clinical experience, time and again we have run into clinical situations where our patients suffer from complexes, illnesses, dysfunctional behaviors, and troubled relationships in sharp contrast to the adequate parenting and nurturing environment that their adoptive parents have provided. In most of these instances, we have found that the presenting picture did not make sense in the context of the individual's upbringing and environment. We were forced to dig deeper to find yet another missing piece of the jigsaw puzzle. To our surprise, the picture would fall into place when we factored in the personalities of their biological parents. While consciously our patients had identified with their often healthy adoptive parents, unconsciously these individuals had been burdened by the unresolved karma of their biological parents and their ancestors.

Jerry's Gambling Addiction

Jerry works as an air-traffic controller, a notoriously high-stress job. From early on, he knew he had been adopted by the man and woman he called mom and dad. His early life developed with only the normal and expectable difficulties of growing up, of school, peers, adolescence, and job training. The mate Jerry chose likewise worked a high-stress job. Their married life progressed satisfactorily for several years with only the usual struggles a young married couple faces. At one point, however, Jerry got a promotion and another huge dose of stress. Concurrently, his wife became concerned about Jerry's health and well-being. Jerry attempted to manage both his new position, his increased stress, and his wife's worries by, of all things, starting to gamble.

His adoptive parents racked their brains, trying to understand whether or where they had failed their son. They consulted therapists; Jerry went into treatment for gambling addiction; but nothing seemed to make sense or alleviate his addiction. The situation got worse. Jerry began loosing ever larger sums of money, which he tried to conceal from his wife. But of course, she found out and confronted him. She said she couldn't live with a liar and a gambler; and Jerry said he couldn't stop gambling. They decided to divorce.

Jerry, like many adopted children, had always been curious about his birth parents. He was able to find the records of his adoption, and subsequently learn about his birth mother and father. What he discovered was that his father, too, had attempted to deal with excessive and prolonged stress by gambling. Jerry's gambling addiction was not only his own, but his father's, as well. Jerry's parents had given him up for adoption; his birth father and mother had divorced; and his father, unable to cure his addiction, had eventually committed suicide. Jerry now understood that his gambling addiction had roots that extended beyond himself. Knowing this likewise helped him understand that his anxious response to excessive stress was partly a legacy from his biological father. That is, the family karma from his father amplified Jerry's current level of stress. This knowledge helped Jerry detach to some extent from his current problems, and learn more healthful ways of managing stress.

At the recommendation of his therapist, Jerry took up yoga, which he began to practice not only every morning before he went to work, but during the day when he felt stressed. He now has an active support system with his fellow yoga practitioners, Gamblers Anonymous, and his sponsor, who has helped him work out some of his issues relating to his birth father and his adoption. Happily, he has now contained his temptation to gamble.

When people who have been adopted see that they have been unconsciously carrying the unretired family karma of their biological ancestors, their own problems finally make sense. It is our speculation that the adoption experience may have been arranged by the universe as the only method to break the vicious cycle of the biological ancestor's karma. Had these children been raised by their biological parents, it is very probable that they could have gotten much sicker and more troubled. So the adopted children, though traumatized sometimes by feelings of perceived abandonment, are also in a unique position to recognize and retire the toxic karma of their biological ancestors, and heal the curse of the clan.

Women and men who were adopted as infants or children and choose to research their biological ancestry face some challenges that other adults do not. However, in recent years, the laws and restrictions governing access to adoption records have been relaxed in many states, so don't despair if you were adopted and want to find out more about your biological ancestors.

The first place to start may be with your adoptive parents, if they are open to discussing your adoption. If you cannot obtain any information from them, for whatever reason, you might then consult your local public library, a genealogical society, or Maureen Alice Taylor's *All About Adoption Research* on the Internet, where she offers "some tips and techniques for ferreting out the details of an adoption when they aren't readily available."[2] Another resource, unfortunately rather expensive, is Jayne Askin's *Search: A Handbook for Adoptees and Birthparents*. Askin offers "creative ways to overcome obstacles and attack problems that occur during the search process," and "examines advances that have been made in the area of electronic search methods."[3] (See also Appendix B for more information on genealogical research.)

RELATIONSHIP PATTERNS AND PROBLEMS

Many people have told us that they regretfully recognize they are doing and saying the same things their mother or their father said and did, or that they have married their mother or father. Here we see that the relationship choices we make are not free from our parents' and grandparents' unretired karma. Whatever relationship karma they create and cannot quite retire in their lifetimes becomes a karmic debt for their children who repeat their ancestors' problems. But they also have the opportunity to redeem that karma by working out the relationship issues. On the other hand, parents who have a healthy, respectful, caring, and mutually satisfying relationship in which they are able to resolve their differences and problems often pass that karmic gift on to their children who in turn have a better chance at a successful relationships.

Mindy and Ron

With dedication and hard work, couples can retire personal and family relationship karma. Mindy and Ron are one such couple. They had been married for nearly 20 years when each entered individual therapy.

Neither of their parents' marital relationships gave Mindy and Ron a good basis for founding their own family. Mindy's father was a strict disciplinarian who ruled the roost at home. He could always find fault with Mindy and her brother, but seldom a word of encouragement or praise. Although Mindy knew that Dad had been hard on her and her brother, she often could not recognize his cutting criticism when he was inflicting it on her. Mindy developed both a protective shell around herself, as well as a tendency to criticize others—especially Ron—in the same way her father had criticized her.

Ron's parents had always told him they didn't care what he did so long as he did his best. They may have intended their words to offer acceptance and support, but Ron usually felt that he could always do better. He seldom experienced a deep connection with his parents: Dad would come home from work, install himself in his favorite chair, and read the paper; Mom was busy keeping the home in order. At school, Ron was grateful when other kids let him hang out with them, although he usually felt lonely, like an outsider whom they tolerated. The one area where Ron had some control was studies, which he pursued diligently but alone. He and Mindy met in high school; neither had dated anyone else, and they married shortly after graduation.

Mindy and Ron brought their family karma into their marriage. Mindy feared criticism (like she had experienced from her father), as well as criticized others in the same way her father had criticized her, thereby protecting herself in a relatively impenetrable shell. Ron was devoted to Mindy, longed for deep connection, and "tried to do his best." However, in straining to do his best, he alternated between a degree of attentiveness that Mindy found burdensome, and a defensive insistence that what he did was beyond reproach.

In individual therapy, Mindy began to realize how damaging her father's unrelenting criticism had been: to protect herself, she had developed a shell that excluded Ron; and to keep others at a distance, she had learned to criticize them just as her father had criticized her. Recognizing her legacy from her father was painful, because if she were to shed her shell and criticize less, other people—especially Ron—would probably get closer to her, and that would signal the possibility of her getting hurt emotionally.

In his therapy, Ron was appalled by two insights. First, he more clearly saw how his dependence on acceptance by other people—especially by Mindy—undercut his authentic self-expression. Second, because of his fragile sense of himself, his insisting that he was right shut out other people and increased his loneliness. Ron's legacy from his parents—alternating between subservience and insistence that his way was right (i.e., "the best")—stood in the way of his getting what he really wanted: deep connection with Mindy.

Mindy and Ron worked hard with their individual therapists. Gradually but steadily their relationship improved. Each found the other more accessible, more understanding. Their level of intimacy—emotionally, sexually, spiritually—deepened as they continued to retire the crippling legacies from their parents, their family karma.

EXAMINING OUR PARENTS' AND RELATIVES' RELATIONSHIPS

The traditional family therapy paradigms explore the relationship of the patient with his or her current nuclear family and try to understand it in the context of family of origin. The main emphasis here is to assess how dysfunctional parental relationship is mirrored in the individual's difficulties in his or her personal and professional relationships.

In our analytic focus, time and again we have run into a roadblock when trying to use this approach. Often the patient's parents had good, healthy, functional relationships. Urged on by the patient's dream material and other symptomatic indications, we zoomed in with our analytic microscope to yet a deeper level of inquiry into the family dynamic. What we found was that many of our patients' relational and intrapsycic difficulties were a mirror image of their grandparents' and great-grandparents' psychological problems and unresolved karma going several generations back. We were awed by the biblical prediction that the sins of the parents visited the children for up to four generations and beyond.

The crucial role that grandparents may play in generating family karma for several generations downstream places considerable moral responsibility on the present generation. It mandates that we retire our karmic problems in this lifetime lest we leave the unwanted karmic debt for our grandchildren and great grandchildren, hardly the kind of legacy we want to leave behind. To deal with our psychological problems and spiritual dilemmas becomes more than a luxury for a few worried well-meaning people, but rather an urgent responsibility that we all bear for the future generations.

One of the most significant ways we encounter our universe is through relationships. Good relationships nurture our soul, and conflicted relationships burden our soul. (If you're not sure what sorts of relationships nurture or burden your soul, review chapter 4, pages 36–40, where we discuss the importance of relationships for our soul's growth.) Just as our body needs food, air, and water for nurture, our soul needs nurturing relationships in order to blossom. However, when we ingest polluted air or water, we injure our bodies. When we get caught in toxic relationships, they injure our soul. Why do many intelligent, rational individuals who often spend considerable time and energy in courtship before making commitment to relationships still end up on a dead-end street? Such individuals often go through repetitive cycles of dysfunctional relationships in spite of their personal best judgment. What is the dynamic of this repetition compulsion?

Relationships are an important area where we can work on inherited family karma. Close relationships bring out both the best and the worst in us. They can be a crucible in which our intense emotional fire transforms us, and where we discover ancestral interpersonal patterns that may not be appropriate for us now.

Family karma very often manifests in intimate and work relation-ships, either when we chose a replica of a parent or grandparent, or what looks like their opposite. But both the look-alike and the noth-ing-like turn out to be related as two sides of the same coin: the con-scious personality of the other and that other person's shadow side. Then we realize—much to our dismay—that we have married or are working for one or the other of our parents or some other ancestor; that our partner, co-worker, or boss is a fair copy of Mom or Dad, Grandmother or Grandfather. Unfortunately, some people cycle through this pattern more than once in the hope of developing satisfy-ing love and work relationships.

Journal Exercise: Exploring Relationship Patterns and Family Karma

Take some time to explore your primary relationship. If you are not currently in a relationship, use this exercise to examine your most meaningful past relationship.

A: Functionality

Review the following list of attitudes and behaviors. Underline or circle those terms that characterize your primary relationship. (You may think of additional pairs of qualities you want to add to our list.)

harmony	disharmony
mutuality	self-centeredness
respect	disrespect
sexual satisfaction	lack of sexual satisfaction
cooperation	control
work well together	do not work well together
closeness	distance
shared interests	few/no shared interests
enjoyment of each other	little enjoyment of each other
agreement on fundamental values	no agreement on fundamental values

tolerance for differences   no/little tolerance for differences
loyalty   betrayal
overall satisfaction   dissatisfaction

B: Your Parents' and Grandparents' Relationships

Using the same list of attitudes and behaviors, assess your parents' and your grandparents' relationships, so far as you know about them. There may be some areas where you are not sure. In those instances, other relatives may be able to supply useful information. Family photo albums as well as family stories and legends are often helpful sources.

C: Similarities and Differences

You have probably noticed similarities and differences—family themes and habits and attitudes—as you worked through the exercises in sections A and B. Jot down your observations in your journal. Also note your unanswered questions, your speculations, your guesses.

D: You and Them

Compare your love choices with what you have found out about your parents and grandparents.

• Whom among your forbears do you appear to resemble in your love choices and patterns?
• Compared to your parents and grandparents, what are the areas in which your primary relationship is the worse, the same, or better than theirs?
• Identify the aspects of your love relationship that you choose to work on.

E: Monitor Your Progress

We suggest you keep a list of attitudes, behaviors, and situations in your love relationship that you want to improve, such as in the sample on page 116. Chart your progress daily. This way, you will both remind yourself to pay attention to what you want to change, and be able to see how well you are doing.

Daily Progress Chart: My Relationship

	Sun.	Mon	Tue.	Wed.	Thu.	Fri.	Sat.
1. Harmony/disharmony	+	−	+				
2. Respect/disrespect	+		+				
3. Cooperation/control	+	−					
4. Work well/do not work well	+						
4. Sexual satisfaction/lack of	+						
6. Mutuality/self-centeredness	+	−	+				
7.							
8.							
9.							

Notes

<u>Sunday</u> *was a great day! We got along wonderfully. Don't know how it happened. Everything seemed to go so smoothly.*

<u>Monday</u> *we had some disagreements. Not very harmonious. I felt I had to get some things done, so I didn't pay much attention to anybody else. Kind of self-centered, so we didn't cooperate very well, either. Need to work on making my needs known more clearly and taking others into account.*

<u>Tuesday</u> *I made it a point to pay more attention, be more respectful. I felt a lot more harmony between us, and it felt like neither of us was so self-centered.*

A glance at the table will show you how you are doing: where you are making progress, where you are falling short of the changes you want to make.

CAREER CHOICES

Even if you have chosen something very different from what other members of your family do for a living, it is important to remember what you were feeling as you made your career choice. Sometimes people choose lines of work that are very different from what parents, siblings, and grandparents have chosen, but it can be more of a protest than an authentic choice, an act of rebellion, or self-assertion seeking to break out of a family pattern. Authentic choices may differ from what our relatives do, but when we make an authentic choice, we are listening to the whispers of our soul, not defying what we feel to be someone else's control over us.

Journal Exercise: Examining the Authenticity of Your Career Choice

In your journal, write down your reflections on the following questions:

1. How did you arrive at your career choice?

2. What did you perceive as "family expectations" for you?

3. Is your job satisfactory and does it nurture you, or does it deplete you by the end of the day?

4. Do you look forward to going to work most mornings, or do you eagerly await weekends and vacations?

5. Consider your parents', siblings', and grandparents' careers. How do you rate their job satisfaction compared to yours? Are you in a similar job, related job, or a totally different job compared to them?

FANTASIES

Fantasy offers us the most direct access to what is going on in the psyche outside of our waking consciousness. A fantasy might take the form of a tune we cannot get out of our minds; a pesky thought that won't go away; a word we keep involuntarily repeating; a scene from TV or a film that keeps coming to mind. Whatever form it might take, this sort of involuntary fantasy may be a karmic indicator.

Ernie's Tooth Fantasy

Ernie was interested in art history. He enjoyed his college courses and was looking forward to being an art historian. There was considerable pressure from his parents for him to pursue dentistry as a profession, a subject which held little interest for him. Ernie had a recurring fantasy of a jaw with 32 large teeth chasing him and trying to bite him to pieces. In therapy, we made an interesting discovery: he remembered his grandfather as a critical man who had put Ernie's father down. Grandfather had a "biting" presence about him, just like a mouth full of big, sharp teeth. Ernie learned through the grape vine that grandfather had tried, unsuccessfully, to pursue a dental career, and was bitter about not being able to do so. Instead, he became the biting teeth himself. Ernie now understood the pressure from his parents to pursue dental training.

Journal Exercise: What Do Your Fantasies Reveal?

Hopefully, Ernie's example reminded you of a fantasy which may have persisted in your mind at some time in your life or does so now.

1. Be completely honest and write down your fantasy, using the present tense. Let any detail that comes to mind flow to the page, unedited. Put it aside for a day or so.

2. After you've let your fantasy "rest," read it and circle the primary elements, people, and emotions in the fantasy.

3. Try to relate to each circled item as a symbol of something in your life or your parents' or grandparents' lives. Write down your associations to the words you circled.

4. Which of the elements you discovered in your fantasy are realistically operating in your life now? What elements "belong" to someone else in your family?

5. Imagine how you can now release or change the dynamics revealed in your fantasy.

COMPLEXES

The psyche organizes what it perceives as related emotional experiences into memory units that we call "complexes." As such, complexes are natural and normal features of our emotional make up. However, when a complex takes on a life of its own—that is, becomes autonomous and no longer responsive to conscious control—*it* has *us*. We can have all kinds of pleasant as well as pesky, troublesome, embarrassing memories and complexes.

Our memories and our complexes—both pleasant and painful—cluster around one or more emotions. Anything associated with a given experience may trigger the emotions that hold a specific memory complex together. Often the emotion is what we first experience, but we may not know the content to which it refers. When we reflect on the emotion, we may be able to access the memory associated with it, and then discover the connection between the present trigger stimulus and the experience.

For example, we want to remember happy events in life—a fine vacation; a surprise party in our honor; a wedding or birth of our child—so we keep something to remind us. The reminder may be a souvenir, a favor from the party, photographs, and the like. The purpose of the reminder is to re-access the original complex of experience and activate the memory of the occasion. Although pleasant memory complexes usually do not take on a life of their own (i.e., become independent of our conscious control), they can when we want to escape a present situation. Unpleasant complexes usually form around emotional wounds and areas in which we feel inadequate or inferior. When something reminds us of the unpleasant or wounding experience or situation—that is, activates that particular complex—we feel as though the original experience is happening to us all over again.

Complexes intrude into our conscious life. Their intrusion ranges from subtle to gross, interfering in one way or another with what we are doing. For example, we may make a "slip of the tongue," saying exactly the inappropriate thing for the situation. We may stammer, or be at a loss for words in the presence of certain people, or appear at the wrong time for some occasion we didn't really want to attend anyway. Often these are relatively inconsequential "lapses," yet they are sure evidence that we are not masters in our own psychological house, and they are worthy of our exploration.[4]

Complexes manifest most blatantly as emotional eruptions that coerce and obsess us to a greater or lesser extent, and resist our conscious control. When the emotion erupts, we fell as though we are going to "lose it," "fly off the handle," "go ballistic." Typically we blame the situation or the other person: "It's all his/her fault that I'm so upset and out of control!" "That ruined my whole day."

Our personal complexes develop in the course of our life, especially our early years. In part, some of our complexes take shape around our innate disposition: each of us is born with a unique mix of typically human potentials. In that mix, some potentials are stronger, some weaker. Typically, we develop our stronger talents and try to ignore our weaker ones. The morphogenic fields of our family make it easier to learn family patterns than to develop in original ways. We often adapt our talents to the family model. Consequently, our gifts that fit well with family patterns become stronger while our innate potentials for which we receive no support go underground. You can see why it is sometimes so difficult to be oneself.

Complexes grow stronger through repeated experiences that reinforce them. This holds true for complexes that we experience as positive as well as negative. For example, we can develop a mini-complex around some insignificant irritant, such as an advertisement on radio or TV that interrupts the program we are wanting to follow. This is harmless, but the experience typifies the nature of the complex: we don't have full control over our reaction. At times, however, this harmless anger complex may have deeper roots, for instance, chronic feelings of hurt and loss of control in dealing with an intrusive parent.

With a little work, we can usually identify personal complexes since they arose in the course of our life, and we have memories of events, actions, and circumstances in which they originated and that reinforced them. Family complexes, however, lack the clear, personal basis. Family complexes have a "just so" quality: we experience them as if they are part of the way things are, the way the world is. We take them for granted. Sometimes we don't even think of questioning them. We were born into them rather than developed them in the course of our lives. Not only do we inherit our ancestors' genes, so that we look or walk or talk like Uncle Bill or Grandma, we can also inherit some of their emotional sensitivities and vulnerabilities, their attitudes, their values and prejudices. In other words, the morphogenic fields of our parents' and our grandparents' complexes can shape corresponding complexes in us.

If we follow the history of our personal complexes, and trace them back to our parents and grandparents, we start to identify the threads that weave the carpet of our personality. When a complex erupts blatantly, our behavior changes in four typical ways: our adaptation regresses to that of an earlier developmental level; we become more emotional; we blame the other for "making" us react; and our emotions tend to rumble about inside us for a long time. This "something" that awakens a complex may cause acute discomfort in the present and remind us of a past experience. It may be an embarrassing encounter with someone, a missed opportunity, or some thoughtless word or deed that caused another person pain. The present event accesses both the emotion and the content of the memory. We have no doubt about the connection: this is personal complex material. A handy way to remember the four major complex indicators is to use the mnemonic "REPP-ertory" of the complex's behaviors.

Regression

The "R" in "REPP-ertory" refers to regression. When a complex seizes us, our behavior "regresses" to a more primitive, less adapted level. We have all seen this in children (not to mention adults). When a child tries to do something at the edge of his or her ability, fails, and feels shame, the child often then starts to behave in a manner younger than his or her years. What often happens when an adult experiences some significant setback or failure is that the individual says, "I'll never try that again!" And doesn't! In other words, the individual—child or adult—goes back to a way of behaving prior to attempting to do what failed. Both adults and children may display regression when stressed. When anxious, the child may revert to thumb sucking, and the adult may regress to sucking a cigarette (or a beer). Regression—R—is one of the observable behaviors in the REPP-ertory.

Emotionality

The "E" refers to emotionality. When we "go ballistic" or "fly off the handle," we experience and express a lot of emotion. This level of emotion is disproportionate to the situation at hand.

For example, one of our friends, Judy, had been working under stressful conditions in an on-line retail business for several months, cleaning up the mess a previous employee had made in cataloguing and describing items in inventory. She believed she had finally eradicated all the traces of the "Curse of Rob," as she called the problems that the former employee had created. One day, she filled an order, billed the customer's charge card, and was getting ready to ship the item. When she inspected it more closely, she saw that it had sustained a "Curse of Rob": the item was in very poor condition, not at all as it had been described. In a moment of sudden rage, she threw the item across the room, then kicked it around. When her emotion was spent, she felt terrible. She realized she had acted like a frustrated child, and that the trigger—the incorrectly inventoried item—was hardly enough to provoke the rage she felt.

As we discussed her outburst, she realized that the item was the proverbial "last straw." What had finally broken out was the accumulated frustration she had endured cleaning up Rob's mess, a mess compounded by the owner's own laziness and inability to confront Rob. In the course of those many months, Judy had not adequately expressed her frustration at both Rob and the owner. Unfortunately, her employer was neither understanding of her frustration nor appreciative of the many months of hard work she had put in getting this aspect of his business cleaned up and in order. Despite her sincere apologies, he fired her the next day.

Projection

The next element is "P"—projection. Projection happens to us when we automatically say, "It's somebody else's fault!" Blaming someone else is a deep-seated human impulse in the service of maintaining self-esteem. When we are in a complex, and overly emotional, the projection helps us drain the excessive affect onto a recipient or scapegoat who somehow hooks into our complex.

Individually, we may blame the spouse, employer, neighbor, parents, and sometimes even strangers (as in road rage) as containers of our projections when we are overwhelmed by emotions released by a particular complex. Collectively, when we experience major catastrophic events or setbacks in society we tend to blame groups like gays, minorities, foreigners, etc., who then become the scapegoats "responsible" for what happened. So "P" refers to projection.

Perseveration

The last "P" is perseveration, which means getting stuck in a vicious circle of emotions and behaviors that feed on each other. We all know that it takes us time to cool off, to get a grip, to get our feet on the ground again, because the emotion of the complex dissipates slowly. We may retell the incident many times, feeling the waves of emotion sweep over us again and again. Only gradually do the emotions abate until we are back to what is normal for us.

HOW TO WORK WITH COMPLEXES

The way you can work effectively with complexes follows directly from the typical features of the complex: the change in your behavior, your increased (often inappropriate) emotion, blaming someone else for setting you off, and recognition that it takes a while to cool down. By paying attention to what you are experiencing you gain personal knowledge, and then you can take responsibility for both your reactions and for corralling the unruly complex. Here are the steps:

1. Recognize when you have become unusually emotional.

2. Identify the current trigger event and your emotions. Write down: a) your emotions; b) your fantasies revolving around the incident; c) your memories of similar experiences (people, places, events).

3. Pinpoint the unresolved issue or undeveloped potential that the complex represents.

4. Imagine a more effective way of dealing with the stimulus that activated the complex. For example, it may just require your recognition, taking a deep breath, and telling yourself to attend to what is actually happening. Using Judy's example, she might have recognized her reaction to the bad cataloging that she missed as activating her accumulated frustration, taken a breath, and consulted with her superior about the problem.

5. Work out a sequence of different behaviors (in increasing order of difficulty) to address the core issue in the complex. Using Judy's example again, by going to her superior with the problem, she is directly working with the complex: accepting that she couldn't catch every single mistake Rob had made *and* enlisting the help of an authority to correct the situation. In the future, instead of giving in to a sense of futility in trying to attain perfection or superiority, she could identify other challenges in her work place that she might take on with her boss's support.

6. Chart your progress by noting non-habitual behaviors to situations and individuals that activate the complex in terms of: increased lead time to choose how to react; more rapid recovery from complex discharge; less frequent activation.

Since complexes are fundamental structural units of the psyche, many aspects of life that we experience have a complex structure: dreams and waking fantasies; fascinations and antipathies; relationship problems; medical and psychiatric conditions; and chakra imbalances. We will now consider techniques for working with several of them.

Stubborn Complexes

In our clinical practice, time and again we have run into individuals who have struggled with stubborn complexes that make no sense in terms of their personal experience in this lifetime. These may take the form of gambling or drug addiction, persistent relationship difficulties (such as cheating on their spouse), or professional obstacles such as irresponsibility or lack of motivation. When an assessment of these individuals' earlier lives and childhood experiences under the analytic microscope has yielded dwindling returns, we have turned our analytic focus onto the legacy of their clan and their ancestors, and it has yielded handsome dividends. In these instances, such unexplained complexes resonate with similar problems in ancestors, dating several generations back.

For example, Alexandra (whom we discussed in chapter 4) carried the heavy burden of her ancestors' suffering in Russia. Her own family beginnings and the desperate families she worked with as a social worker were very much like many of the first generation Russian immigrants to the U.S.: forced to live in ghettos, barely able to make ends meet; plagued with alcohol abuse.

Alexandra behaved as though she herself were an immigrant, forced to live in a ghetto, struggling to survive in a foreign land. But the "family" she was keeping alive was not her blood family; rather, it was her social work client families with whom she identified as with her own ancestors. Seeing the plight of her client families, she felt survivor guilt and endless, unrelenting responsibility for them.

When she recognized her identification with her clients, she was able to overcome her excessive sense of responsibility and burden of survivor guilt. This, in turn, released a lot of energy formerly in her responsibility and survivor-guilt complex, energy she could now use not only to help her clients, but also to lead a personally more fulfilling, guilt-free life.

Obsessions and Compulsions

Obsessions are persistent ideas, images, or impulses that we experience as intrusive and troubling (e.g. thoughts about contamination; repeated doubts, such as wondering whether one has locked the door; aggressive or horrifying impulses). Compulsions are repetitive behaviors or mental events over which we have no control (such as hand-washing, or silently repeating words), the purpose of which is usually to reduce anxiety. At some point the person suffering from obsessions or compulsions (or both, since they tend to go together) realizes that they are excessive or unreasonable.

Mack's Hand-Washing Compulsion

Mack is a 48-year-old professional who consulted for symptoms of anxiety, depression, and hand-washing. He would wash his hands 60 to 80 times a day, but particularly before touching his children and before shaking hands with colleagues. He had never succeeded to the level that his innate talents and fine training would lead one to expect. Nor could Mack permit himself to purchase the quality clothing or car that his degree of success would permit.

Mack's father and brothers were all involved in a highly successful family construction business. They had created a veritable empire, but they had done so ruthlessly. Mack did not subscribe to those kinds of corporate practices. He started his own one-man construction business.

A few months into therapy, Mack had the following dream:

> *I am looking out of the window of a house overlooking an alley. I see a strong but old man, wearing a dark coat and a hat, slithering into the dark alley. Suddenly, he comes up behind this other man, and stabs him in the back. He carefully wipes his knife and*

puts it back in his coat, quickly looks around, and slips away in
the darkness. Just as he is about to disappear, a car passes nearby
and its headlights catch the killer's face. I am horrified to recog-
nize the killer as my grandfather.

In associating to the dream, Mack reported some family rumors that his
grandfather had had underworld connections and would beat up his
competitors to secure business. There were even very hushed-up stories
that he had put out contracts to threaten people into submission. None
of this had ever been confirmed, and Grandfather had never talked
much about his early years in business. Although Grandfather had been
dead for several years, Mack remembered that as a child, he never felt
comfortable around Grandfather. Grandfather's checkered past had left
scars on Mack's soul.

In the sessions following Mack's reporting this dream, we explored
how Mack had felt when and after he had visited Grandfather. Over
time it became apparent that Mack's hand-washing compulsion was his
attempt to wash away his grandfather's karma and the violent legacy of
his family.

Obsessions and compulsions are classified as anxiety disorders.[5]
Obsessive thoughts, which may not be conscious, create anxiety. In
order to alleviate the anxiety, the obsessively anxious individual engages
in compulsive acts in an attempt to bind the anxiety. Typically, other
people notice the obsessive-compulsive symptoms before the afflicted
individual does. When the individual starts to realize that her or his
thoughts and ideas are obsessive and the consequent behavior is compulsive, it is possible to start looking for the underlying sources of anxiety. However, overcoming obsessions and compulsions on one's own is
next to impossible since we can't see ourselves as clearly as others can
see us. If you suffer from obsessions and compulsions, it is best to seek
competent professional help.

FASCINATIONS AND ANTIPATHIES

Whenever we experience fascination or antipathy, we are reacting to a reflection of some part of our soul that we have not adequately integrated into our conscious personality. Attraction tells us that we want what we see; repulsion tells us the opposite. Either way, our soul is responding to a reflection of our unintegrated potential.

For one reason or another, we have not made this unlived potential part of our conscious life. A fascination or antipathy is a signal from our soul that the present situation offers optimal conditions for incarnation of this potential. We do not fully control this fascination or antipathy, this attraction or repulsion, since it emanates from the depths of our soul rather than from our waking consciousness. The fascination or antipathy can be in response to another person, an idea, a possible experience, a memory, etc. The list is nearly inexhaustible.

Journal Exercise: Working with Fascinations and Antipathies

A: Content and Emotion

Get the facts. Carefully write down the emotions and the content you experience. Every detail may be significant, so do not edit, and do not yet elaborate. For example, the emotion might be irritation at someone in your immediate family or a co-worker:

Alex calls on the phone and starts talking at me without asking whether I have time to talk just then.

B: Review Emotion and Content

Systematically review each emotion and content element. Write down what spontaneously comes to mind.

- What or whom does the image remind you of? Where or with whom have you felt these emotions?
- How was or is this image or emotion significant in your life?
- What role did the image or play in your life in the past?

Continuing with the example in "A:"

Irritation. *Makes me feel disrespected. Taken for granted. Like I am just there to absorb whatever is thrown at me.*

Irritation. *I hate to be interrupted by the phone. People just seem to believe they can call at all hours and start blabbing without ever asking if it's ok with me.*

Irritation. *Reminds me how kids I went to school with always took advantage of me because I would listen to them.*

Letting others overwhelm me actually happens a lot.

C: Visualize How You Would Like to Be

Visualization is a power exercise that prepares you for action by laying the emotional foundation and creating a modified or new morphogenic field.

I will politely interrupt Alex and tell him I am not available when I don't have time to talk. I will also tell Alex to please ask before jumping in and burying me in chatter.

Let your visualization work on you until you can feel how it would be to live what you are visualizing.

D: List and Prioritize the Steps

Identify and prioritize the steps you can take toward the modified or new emotion and behavior. It is often easier to "sneak up" on the big issue by practicing in relatively safer situations and with people where you don't feel a lot is at stake.

1. When telemarketers call, tell them right away I'm not available to talk with them.

2. Stop putting up with people interrupting me in mid-sentence. Tell them I'm not done saying what I wanted to.

3. Sometime when we're together, tell Alex I would appreciate being asked whether I can talk or if another time would be better.

4. When Alex calls and starts to dump on me, say I'm not available then, but would be later, and set a time.

E: Monitor Your Progress

Again, you can chart your progress as you did in the exercise on relationship patterns and family karma, using a table and additional notes, as in the example below.

Daily Progress Chart: Behavior/Emotion Modification

	Sun.	Mon.	Tue.	Wed.	Thu.	Fri.	Sat.
1. Junk Phone calls			+++				
2. Interruptions	-						
3. Tell Alex		-		+			
4. When Alex calls					+		

Notes

Sunday. *Didn't do very well. Went to the mall and the salesclerk hardly would let me get a word in edgewise. Felt really crappy.*

Monday. *Saw Alex, but couldn't get up the courage to say anything. Real irritated. This has got to stop!*

Tuesday. *Phone solicitation. I only listened a couple of minutes, then said I wasn't interested. Probably was a bit more emotional than I needed to be, but got off the phone pretty quick.*

Wednesday. *Saw Alex. Said, "When you call, I'd appreciate your asking if I can talk right then." I was surprised that Alex took it ok.*

Thursday. *Call about suppertime from Alex, who started to chat without asking me. After a couple of minutes, I said, "Alex, I'm eating dinner now, I'll call you back in an hour." Alex was surprised, but said "OK."*

PSYCHIATRIC AND MEDICAL CONDITIONS
AND CHAKRA IMBALANCES

Some of what we inherit from our family lineage is genetic, e.g., body type, hair and skin coloration, vulnerability to some chronic and degenerative diseases. However, family morphogenic fields and parental example shape many of our attitudes, behaviors, and emotions, and can get us into lifestyles that trigger physical and mental health problems.

Many psychiatric and medical symptoms have a clear-cut karmic context when we reflect on their possible meaning. When we can understand them as information at more than one level—that is, not only anatomically or physiologically—they can reveal a karmic past that leads us to our path to the soul. For instance, an individual who is burning with ambition in the first half of life, driven by the pursuit of power and success, may manifest stomach ulcer, or worse, stomach cancer in his or her 40's, 50's, or 60's. The "fire in the belly" (unrestrained ambition, the expression of an unbalanced third chakra) burns a hole in the gut, on the one hand alerting the person to a psychic life out of control like a runaway train, and on the other, holding out the possibility of redeeming life by undertaking appropriate changes. If such an individual retires the stomach ulcer karma, not only will he or she be better able to control the symptoms, but also to open his or her life to new and creative possibilities to live out of the soul.

Margaret's Liver Cancer

Margaret had been a teacher all her life, and all her life she had suffered what she called "liver upsets" and "sick headaches:" from time to time she would experience severe abdominal pain and indigestion so severe that she could not take any food. The only thing that helped was bed rest and withdrawal from her usual activities.

After she retired from teaching, Margaret's recently widowed sister came to live with her, "temporarily." However, the "temporary" arrangement extended into several years. Although her sister's presence distressed her, Margaret couldn't bring herself to tell her sister she had to find a place of her own. This time her life-long inability to say "no" did not lead to a "liver upset" and a "sick headache," but to liver cancer.

Although Margaret received state-of-the-art medical treatment, she could not do the necessary psychological work: she could not gain enough self-esteem to set necessary limits and protect her boundaries. Margaret died and her sister continued to live in Margaret's home for another year and a half before it was sold.

We can understand Margaret's liver cancer from the viewpoint of chakra balance and imbalance. Although she had indeed survived the Great Depression of the 1930s and the difficulties of World War II as a single mother, her root support and foundation—first chakra—was actually weak. She did not feel safe and secure. Her tendency to hoard (every drawer and cabinet was full to overflowing) betrayed her survival anxiety. Often she felt she was a victim. Lacking a solid first-chakra foundation that would have provided her a sense of assured survival, she experienced subtle fear and lack of self-confidence in stressful situations. Since it was frequently difficult for her to affirm herself and her needs (a second-chakra function and task), she often felt martyred.

Margaret's "liver upsets" directly related to her third chakra corresponding to all digestive organs: stomach, intestines, liver, gallbladder, and spleen. When she reached her limit of feeling herself as the victim, martyr, and drudge, the unbalanced energy of her third chakra found expression somatically as a "liver upset." Since she could not consciously, voluntarily, and appropriately express assertive, self-protective anger and take actions that would define and defend her limits, liver cancer was her body's way of finally extricating her from an intolerable situation.

Sylvia's Voices

One of our patients, Sylvia, had long suffered from auditory hallucinations: She heard Satan's voice inviting her to join him and to relinquish her connection with Christ. Psychiatrically, Sylvia's condition would be diagnosed as chronic schizophrenia. Sylvia was a married woman with three adult daughters who had left home and were well-established in their lives. Her husband was committed and attentive, and had cared for her through sickness and health. The content of her hallucinations was puzzling: What might be their karmic root? Once Sylvia started to trust me as a therapist, she related the following story that, to my amazement, gave her hallucinations a clear karmic context.

Sylvia was raised as a devout Christian by conservative and devoted parents. At age 17, she became pregnant. Because of her religious background, abortion was not an option, and because she felt she had let her parents down, she could not share her dilemma with them. She also felt she could not ask for God's help when she had sinned. She said that, in her desperation, she turned in her fantasies to Satan for help. Two weeks later, she had a spontaneous miscarriage, and the incident was "forgotten" (i.e., split off, dissociated from consciousness).

However, deep in her psyche was rooted the idea that she had surrendered her first-born into Satan's custody. In her therapy, she said she hoped that Satan was taking good care of her lost child. As she worked through the pain of her loss and grief, the intensity of her hallucinations gradually diminished. Her action—pregnancy out of wedlock, and turning to Satan for help—brought the consequence of schizophrenic hallucination! When she worked through her grief and accepted what she had done, she was able to forgive herself. Then her hallucinations subsided. She reconnected with her children, her spouse, and now her grandchildren.

In Sylvia's case, acting on a second-chakra drive—sexual activity and her pregnancy—and her religious beliefs interacted to produce her intense guilt, isolation, and ultimately the hallucinations. Although she had reared her three daughters, who were well-established in their adult lives, and her husband was caring and loyal, Sylvia's individuation and spiritual growth was on hold.

Hallucinations may occur in any sensory modality. A person may experience weird tastes or sensations, hear voices, or see "things that aren't there." A hallucination is not always a product of a brain or neurological disorder; it can be a psychological phenomenon related to a person's inability to accept some aspect of his or her self that is loathsome and hence detached from consciousness.

If you have been experiencing hallucinations, it is important for you to seek professional help to identify the source of the hallucination, what it is trying to tell you, and how to deal with it. Start with a psychiatric consultation to rule out neurological and biochemical issues; only then work on the psychological and karmic dimension.

Medical and psychiatric conditions are our soul's most urgent distress calls; they are often accompanied by emotional issues; and all three frequently correlate with chakra imbalances. If you are experiencing physical symptoms (e.g., shortness of breath or difficulty breathing; dizziness; chest pains; chronic headaches; blood in your urine or stool; etc.), or recurrent bouts of depression, anxiety, hallucinations, loss of a sense of passing time, or severe relationship difficulties, you should consult your primary physician and ask for treatment or referral.

It is important to inform your primary caregiver of your lifestyle, because the way you live significantly influences not only the quality of your living but may also affect the length of your life. Medical and psychiatric symptoms are a final distress call to alert us to the danger of suffocating, alienating, or losing our soul. On the other hand, if we respond to this call, we have a chance to cross the bridge that leads us back to the soul.

Chakra Imbalances

In chapter 5, and just now in the cases of Margaret and Sylvia, we have seen how family karma can settle in the chakras, resulting in energy imbalances that manifest in emotion, behavior, medical, and/or psychiatric conditions. Our discussion of the chakras and chakra imbalances has not been exhaustive. But we hope you have gotten some sense of the chakras and how significant they are in the economy of a healthy body and psyche. Hopefully, you were able to find clues as to whether you have a chakra imbalance and where it is. Self-knowledge is the first step to healing.

Many excellent books teach you how to work on chakra blockages or overactivity, and it's possible to find a professional who specializes in energetic bodywork to help bring your chakras back into balance. Most important in this work, however, is your own realization of your mind-body connection, and your dedication to changing your patterns of relating while you work on your chakra imbalance.

DREAMS

Throughout the ages, people have remembered and told their dreams as valuable communications from another realm. Today we know that all humans, and many of our animal relatives, have dreams. Now people are rediscovering their dreams as crucial sources of guidance "from within." Often our dreams are so vivid that we awake deeply moved, still filled with the emotions we experienced in the dream. Jim, the retired businessman we mentioned in chapter 2, had a dream that illustrates how important dreams can be.

Jim's Dream

In his second therapy session, Jim presented the following dream:

I am at a party. It's a lovely evening with music in the background. My wife looks pretty in her black satin dress. She is dancing with a handsome man at the other end of the hall. I try to catch her attention, unsuccessfully. I retire to my host's study, and log onto the computer chat room, but do not have the password. I feel alone and rejected.

Jim had been a hard-driving businessman up until his retirement. He had this dream on the first morning after retiring. What does it say about Jim's karma? First, we see that he has no connection with his wife. He recognizes her as attractive, but she is dancing with another man at the far end of the hall. Jim cannot get her attention. It does not occur to him in the dream to cut in and dance with her. Instead, he goes off to his host's study to join a virtual reality for which, alas, he doesn't even have the password!

The dream lays out the treasure and the tragedy of his psychic potential. His beautiful wife represents not only the woman to whom he is married, but also that realm of his psyche with which he longs for relationship but from which he is cut off. Her black satin dress suggests allure and the unknown; that is, both Jim's desire for and his ignorance of her, and what she represents of his unknown potential. She is cloaked in his darkness, in his self-centered pursuit of success and power that crushed his tender and precious relationships with wife and children. She is dancing with a handsome, lively, sociable man. Jim initially did not realize that the unknown man was the other man in himself with whom he had lost connection.

Jim's soul work subsequently focused on his retiring his karmic debt of one-sidedness and consciously cutting into the dance with his own emerging potentials as well as learning to cultivate the relationship with his wife. Like many contemporary men and women, Jim had attempted to create a life in limited reality. Modern men and women create their limited realities by acquiring material possessions and pursuing outer success. While possessions and some degree of success are necessary to maintain ourselves in the world as we know it, they constitute a limited reality, and hence merit the label of maya. What is missing from this sort of life is the sense of purpose and value greater than the satisfaction of greed and ambition. The sense of purpose and value, the intimation of where we fit in the larger scheme of things, is the password that connects us with our soul.

Dreams show us how our soul views our life. As a general rule, a dream supplies the information that consciousness either does not have, or does not adequately perceive or value. The following very general rules of thumb will help you orient yourself to your dream.

Dreams often give us hints, point out where we are stuck, and show us new ways of being. Actually, in many dreams we see ourselves doing and saying things we couldn't possibly say or do in waking life. Yet these kinds of dreams offer us a new energy pattern, a new morophogenic template. We can help the new pattern establish itself in our waking life when we regularly recall the healing image and the emotion that accompanies it. (It is very important to experience, to feel, the image.)

Typically, dreams have a recognizable dramatic structure: setting, development, turning point, and resolution. Sometimes one or more of these elements is missing, in which case we have an unfinished dream. Don't worry; from time to time, we all get dreams that are or seem incomplete. We can still work with what we have.

When *known people and places* appear in your dream, they may refer either to the actual people and places, or—more probably—to something in you that resembles those people and places. For example, when your mother or father appears in your dream, the message may be about the mothering or fathering capacity in yourself that your experience of your parents has shaped and left as an inner authority. When a known person or place appears in your dream but differs from reality in some way (age, looks, actions, attitude), you can be pretty sure that the dream is talking about a part of your psyche that functions like that person or place.

One last word: Working on your own dreams is about the process of dream work, not the outcome of the work. It's amazing. The "product" you end up with may not look like much, but the process you have engaged in works on you, and will subtly deepen and inform your consciousness of the intentions of your soul. Here are the basic elements of dream work you need to know; with practice you can acquire the fundamental skills.

WORKING WITH DREAMS

To catch your dreams:

- Keep your dream notebook and pen or pencil next to your bed, or a small tape recorder into which you can narrate your dream.

- When you go to bed, suggest to yourself that you will recall a dream.

- Write down your dream as soon as you are aware of it.

- If your dream slips away as you are waking up, lie still, get back into the same position and posture you were in as you awoke. Often you can recall your dream in this way.

To work with your dreams:

- Review the dream you want to work on. Re-visualize the images; feel the emotions again; re-experience the dream. This brings the dream back to life.

- Contemplate each image. Write down the feelings, memories, and impressions that arise when you hold each image, situation, person, etc., in your mind's eye and in your feelings. *Stay with the image; circle around it; don't let your associations lead you far afield.*

- Consider the structure of your dream. Does it have a setting? Does the action develop? Is there a turning point? Does the dream reach a conclusion? (Often our dreams end before the turning point or the conclusion, which implies that the development cannot go further at the time.)

- What does the dream appear to be commenting on in your life? Some complex? Your relationships? How you get around in the world? The (emotional and mental) space you inhabit? What is opposing or assisting you? Your karmic inheritance?

- Compare your current dream with other dreams in which the same or similar persons, places, themes, and images have appeared. What changes do you notice? How does your presence in the current dream differ from what it was in the past?

- After working on your dream, note how your emotional state has changed in the course of the your dream work.

- Honor your dream by carrying out some action or ritual in your waking life that involves the images and intent of the dream.

- Work with a sensitive friend (or therapist) who can lead you through these steps and keep you focused, but doesn't tell you what your dream means.

TRAGIC EVENTS

Sometimes karma and family karma manifest as tragic events. Recall that karma refers to choices, actions, and the consequences that necessarily follow. The person who performs the acts may harvest some karma in his or her lifetime, but very often the consequences descend upon the children and grandchildren. Not all such events are on the grand scale of the House of Atreus or the Kennedy family's drama. Indeed, many of us suffer the reverberations of ancient and not-so-distant family tragedies.

When something terrible happens, it triggers a great deal of emotion and physiological change that settle in the related chakras, and as we discussed earlier, this energy gets transmitted to other family members who then may find themselves experiencing similar tragedies.

Sarah's Family Tragedy

Sarah's maternal grandfather was a surgeon who had served in both WWII and the Korean War. He had extremely high morals and a hair-trigger temper. He would often fly into a rage and beat his children whenever he felt they were lying or being rude. Sarah's grandmother was remembered primarily as a wife first, mother second, dissolving into the background and existing primarily to keep the peace and please her husband. His temper and stressful work contributed to his death of a stroke early in his 40s. Sarah's mother was seventeen at the time. Sarah's bereaved grandmother became an alcoholic and died some 15 years later of cancer. Sarah's mother, seeking the parental affection she felt she lacked, became pregnant when she was 19 by a man 13 years her senior. He was a flamboyant character, but, like Sarah's grandfather, had a dark side and drank heavily. She divorced him when Sarah was four and later remarried another talented, driven man who died suddenly of a heart attack at 37. And, like Sarah's grandmother, Sarah's mother became an alcoholic after her stepfather died. Sarah has had to seek extensive therapy in order to secure healthy relationships with emotionally stable men, instead of choosing unstable men or ruining a healthy relationship with a self-fulfilling abandonment complex.

Journal Exercise: Dealing with Family Tragedies

Sarah's family karma is certainly tragic: three generations of unstable relationships plagued by hot temper, early death, and alcohol abuse. Not all family karma is tragic as was Sarah's; yet, when dysfunctional attitudes and behaviors repeat generation after generation, we see another kind of tragedy: inherited family karma. As you have worked through the exercises earlier in this book, you have become aware of a lot of "stuff" about yourself and your family. Now is a good opportunity to review and reflect again on some of your family tragedies: those interactive patterns of emotion, action, and consequences that repeat generation after generation.

- List the tragedies in your family history.
- What are the parallels between these events and similar events in your life?

- What are the effects on your relationship patterns?
- What are the effects on your other life choices?
- How have you counteracted the effects of those family tragedies in your life?
- What do you still need to do to counteract the effects of those family tragedies in your life?

◆   ◆   ◆

Complexes, dreams, fascinations and antipathies, relationships, medical and psychiatric conditions provide a lot of information. Now, how do we organize all that we know about ourselves so that we can more clearly trace the strands of family karma interwoven in our lives? Our answer is to construct an annotated family tree, a "genogram." The genogram—the focus of the next chapter—provides a useful way to organize and map what we find out about ourselves and our family patterns.

7

MAPPING YOUR FAMILY KARMA: THE GENOGRAM

A road-map makes the journey easier. A very useful road-map of family karma is the annotated family tree, the genogram. The genogram gives a bird's eye view of the karmic themes binding us to our family.

On a genogram we can note all sorts of significant information besides the usual marriages, divorces, deaths, and births. For example, we can indicate complexes; medical and psychiatric symptoms; the positive and negative interpersonal relationships among generations; the communication styles and transactional patterns; the occupations; the evolution of family myths; illnesses and addictions; and themes, secrets, and losses, to mention only a few of the many possibilities.

BASIC COMPONENTS OF THE GENOGRAM

In constructing genograms, we will use several standard components. Typically, a genogram represents female family members as circles, and males as squares. Conventionally, the square (male) is placed on the left and the circle (female) on the right:

We represent the person on whom we are focusing—the index person—as a double square or circle, with birth dates shown in superscript on the left:

When two people marry, a line with the marriage date connects their geometric representations, and when children are born, they are added with their birth dates:

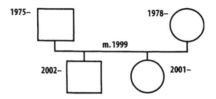

A circle or square with an "X" through it indicates a death:

USING THE GENOGRAM TO MAP FAMILY KARMA

The amount of information you can enter on a genogram is limited only by the size paper you have. In the following examples, we will not attempt to enter all the possible manifestations of family karma. Rather, for the sake of clarity (and the limited size of the printed page!), we will construct genograms of two clients we discussed earlier in the book.

Tom the Concerned, Controlling Father

In chapter 5, we discussed Tom, the very successful but controlling businessman who came for therapy with concerns about his relationship with his son and other important people in his life. Recall that Tom's father was a professionally unsuccessful man who could not make a good living. Consequently, Tom had grown up in situation of financial deprivation, sometimes so bad that his family had to go on welfare to survive. Tom vowed never again to experience that sort of humiliation and need, nor to let any child of his suffer as he had suffered. Tom built a fortune, set up trust funds for each of his children, and retired early in his 50s. Tom's relationship with his son was strained because his son was burning through his trust fund in a failing business venture, and Tom was at his wits end and desperate to save his son from ruin. When we set up a genogram for Tom, his father, and his son, here's what we get (see figure 2 on page 146).

Tom's genogram is relatively simple. The lineage of his need to control is direct. The text boxes on the left of the genogram summarize the significant facts of Tom's and his son's family karma. Note especially the first chakra/third chakra alternation. Tom compensated for his father's impaired first (survival) chakra by overworking his third (authority and control) chakra. In his efforts to protect his son from experiencing first chakra struggles, and by attempting to direct his life, Tom deprived his son of the opportunity to develop his own first-chakra survival skills.

Karen's Sexual Fantasies

Karen, you recall, is the adopted daughter whose mother had attempted to abort her, and whose grandmother had been promiscuous as a young woman. Karen learned of her adoption only as an adult woman. Her occasional sexual fantasies disturbed her greatly because she loved her husband and children. Until she discovered that both her mother and her grandmother had been promiscuous as young women, Karen couldn't understand why she occasionally had sexual fantasies that, if acted on, would jeopardize her marriage and family. Their promiscuity was their attempt to relieve their abandonment anxiety; Karen recognized that she experienced similar anxiety and sexual fantasies. A look at Karen's genogram on page 147 reveals her complicated family karma history.

Karen's genogram is somewhat more involved than Tom's. The genogram concisely summarizes the three-generational fear of abandonment, and Karen's and her mother's desperate attempts to deal with it. Karen's birth parents never married; and her birth mother broke off all contact with Karen. (Notice that two lines are broken by a double

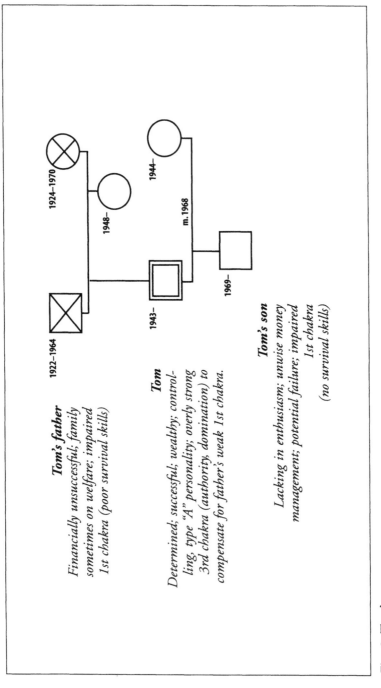

Tom's father

Financially unsuccessful; family sometimes on welfare; impaired 1st chakra (poor survival skills)

Tom

Determined; successful; wealthy; controlling, type "A" personality; overly strong 3rd chakra (authority, domination) to compensate for father's weak 1st chakra.

Tom's son

Lacking in enthusiasm; unwise money management; potential failure; impaired 1st chakra (no survival skills)

1922–1964

1924–1970

1948–

1944–

m. 1968

1943–

1969–

Fig. 2. Tom's genogram.

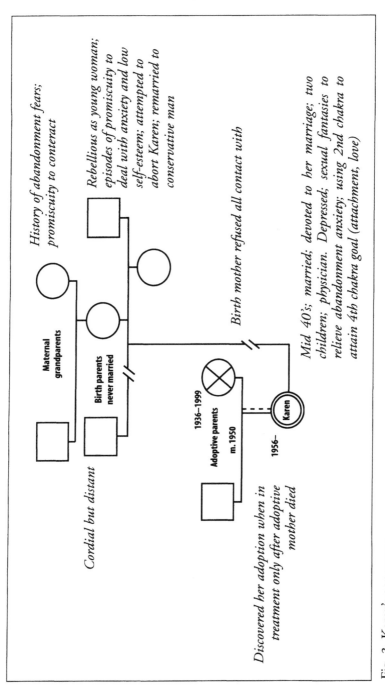

Fig. 3. Karen's genogram.

slash, "//", indicating a break in relationship. The lines connecting Karen and her adoptive parents—one solid and one broken—indicate adoption.)

SETTING UP YOUR GENOGRAM

Throughout this book, we have presented vignettes of persons with whom we have worked who discovered that family karma—blessings and curses from their ancestors—plays a significant role in their life problems: complexes; emotional and relationship issues; subtle imperatives they felt they had to follow; prohibitions they believed they could not violate; addictions that puzzled them. We have seen that family karma affects people like us as well as national icons such as the Kennedy family.

In the preceding chapter, we suggested sources from which you can get information about the history of your family; and in the first part of this chapter we constructed genograms of two of the case vignettes presented earlier in the book that vividly illustrate the persistence of family karma through two or three generations. Now it is your turn to construct the genogram that will help you identify family karmic influences affecting your life here and now. (Consult Appendix B for help with genealogical research.)

Journal Exercise: Your Annotated Genogram

You can set up your genogram on paper or use a computer program designed especially for that purpose. The various Journal Exercises you have already worked through will provide you rich material, and probably provide clues about several gaps in important information that you may want to try to fill in.

A genogram is essentially a "family tree." The convention is to put oneself at the bottom, as a descendant (although real trees grow from the bottom up!), or, if you have children, put them in the bottom row with you just above them. Then start filling in the circles and squares for the men and women, again starting with yourself. Leave plenty of room; by now you have a lot of information. If you take your time and organize what you have found out in the course of this book, you will have a richly informative overview of your karmic inheritance—and your karmic burden!

◆   ◆   ◆

We have considered ancestral curses and blessings as not only problems, which they certainly can be, but also as opportunities for your spiritual growth. The oyster of your personality can take the sand grit of the family karma and incubate the pearl of your innate potential. We have laid out the framework for healing emotions, modifying dysfunctional behavior, cultivating spiritual growth, and transforming the personality by integrating the emerging frontiers of spirituality and mind/body medicine in healing the deep, unconscious, and invisible wounds inflicted by the family toxicity that accumulates in the soul over several generations.

In the next chapter, we will situate your individual effort in the larger, archetypal context.

8

ENCOURAGEMENT FOR YOUR SOUL JOURNEY

In Exodus 20:5 we read that God will punish "the children for the sin of the fathers to the third and fourth generation." Whether or not you believe that God punishes us for what our ancestors did, the fact remains that we inherit consequences for actions we did not perform. This is not a new idea, but an age-old experience as well as a reality we analysts encounter in our clinical work.

Ancestral karma is an archetypal reality. Archetypal is what is ancient and deeply impressed on the psyche.[1] We saw family karma operating in the myth of the House of Atreus, and in the Kennedy dynasty. We have seen family blessings and curses in many of our patients and in ourselves. It's part and parcel of being human because we are a part of the ancestral whole.

To comprehend your roots and to realize your destiny, you must look beyond your individual life and understand your ancestral context in order to make sense of your journey. You cannot understand a river unless you examine the springs on the mountain tops and the valleys that feed it, as well as the marshes and swamps through which it flows on its way to you. You can understand yourself a lot better if you consider yourself an important organ in the ancestral body of consciousness and karma. While it is tempting to take the ostrich position of looking at your individual life as the cause and course of your destiny, a realistic appraisal of your life calls for taking a panoramic view of your ancestral history and how you fit into it.

WHAT DO YOU DO AFTER YOU'VE
IDENTIFIED FAMILY KARMA?

You are not condemned to repeat the history of your ancestors, but first you have to become conscious of family karmic patterns. Once you have identified the blessings and the curses you have inherited, you have the possibility of choice. The best way to break old patterns is to work on establishing new ones. Nature—including human nature—abhors a vacuum.

As pointed out earlier, we need to have awareness, gain knowledge, and take responsibility. The exercises we discussed in the previous chapters further your awareness and increase your knowledge. Taking responsibility means acting appropriately on what you have discovered.

Practice Makes Perfect

Family karma—as manifested in complexes, attitudes, behaviors, relationship patterns, under- or over-achievement, chakra imbalances, and medical and psychiatric conditions—can and does pass from generation to generation. We are born into those legacies that work on us as models to follow or avoid, and as morphogenic fields that shape us powerfully but invisibly. Once you recognize these influences, you have the opportunity to change how you handle them, but change comes only when you have a direction and are willing to do the necessary work.

Working at change means practicing. Practicing means you bridle your fears and act on the information you have gained. Practicing also means you repeat your new behavior or attitude time and again, until you get it right. In this way, you can tame the excesses and make up the deficiencies you have inherited from your parents, grandparents, and other relatives. Thus, you complete their unfinished tasks, and gain the treasure hard-to-attain, which is your authentic self.

Differentiating the self from the bosom of the family and becoming what you can be—individuation—is a life-long project. It means periodically going back into the family and wresting bits of identity out of it, like the hero at the treasure-trove, and fleeing with it intact. Individuation—differentiating yourself from the collective soup of the family consciousness and unconscious—should be an act of exerting great effort and breaking free of others' expectations of you. It can and should be a natural, evolutionary step, even if difficult, even if other people are upset with you. At certain times in life when you feel stuck, trapped, perpetuating a treadmill existence, you may need to go into the family nest and claim more of your self to gain energy for the next phase in life. True individuation is a process, not an event. It is a project never fully completed. Individuation—fully actualizing your potential—requires diligence, consciousness, and courage. Reclaiming the self from the matrix of the family is the task of the hero in each of us. It is an archetypal imperative, a challenge none of us can avoid.

Fear is the enemy. Changing old patterns is usually frightening. The old patterns are at least familiar; you know what to expect, even if it is consistently bad! So you must consider your fears, but not let them rule you. Usually, you have to face the same fear time and again until you have gradually replaced it with a new behavior, a new way of acting and being with which you have become comfortable. This takes practice.

Insight is half of the equation; the other half is action. When you act differently, you become different. Your behavior and your emotions change. Actually, emotion and behavior influence each other. Emotion can move you to take action, or, equally, stop you dead in your tracks. Likewise, what you do—your actions, your behavior—can enliven or deaden you, make you feel better or worse.

Dreams and other forms of inner information are an especially important source of guidance. When a dream, or a series of dreams, offers you healing images, you can strengthen the effect of those images by visualizing and embodying them. In Appendix A we have listed several good resources that will further assist you.

Visualization works with your ability to conjure images in your mind and process your feelings. In your imagination, you focus on how you want to be, not on coercing other people to meet your expectations. In your visualizations, you can create scenarios in which you act as you would like to. Visualizations, like healing dreams, establish new morphogenic templates.

Ritual is likewise important. A deliberate act that honors a dream message or significant insight anchors the new information in the waking world in a physical way. What sort of ritual you perform is up to you. But whatever you do should be something that moves you, some act that touches your emotions. Repeating the visualizations and rituals continues your conscious support of what the dream tells you.

THE ARCHETYPAL PATTERN

Hero myths and legends reveal the archetypal pattern that informs the process of retiring personal and family karma, and furthering self-actualization, or individuation. The nature of the hero—whether female or male—is to face a twofold task: redeem what has grown old and feeble by discovering the source of renewal and vitality.

As redeemer, the mythic hero may have to heal the ailing king, restore fertility to the land, liberate the realm from oppressors, or fulfill some prophecy. Through the redemptive act, however, the hero founds a new order. Frequently the hero of myth or fairy tale becomes the new king. But in the course of fulfilling the twofold challenge—to bring healing to what exists and to found something new—the hero has to face danger, confront opposition, accomplish nearly impossible tasks, and endure loneliness and isolation before achieving the goal that is often imaged as the "treasure hard-to-attain."

The Treasure Hard-to-Attain

In myth and fairy tale, the treasure is often depicted as a hoard of gold or jewels guarded by a monster (often a dragon), or as a princess held captive by a witch, or ogre; or a prince turned into a frog, or monster. Psychologically or spiritually, the treasure that the hero wins is neither gold nor jewels nor the kingdom, but rather the liberation and union with that other part of the self with whom the hero then restores the kingdom, or founds a new order. Attaining the treasure is the precondition for realization of the self, the progressive fulfillment of the innate potential, personal fractal[2] of the divine. Authentic selfhood is hard to attain because of the burden of family karma, as illustrated by the story of the House of Atreus. We cannot be our real selves until we identify, take responsibility for, and free ourselves from, the burdensome legacy of our ancestors.

We all experience urges, impulses, imperatives that we cannot resist. Mythologically, these would be the effects of what the ancients called "the gods:" emotional forces that can propel us relentlessly, like Orestes, unless we recognize that it is we who choose to raise our hands to act on impulse. It is we who choose to utter the words seething within us that express the mood of the gods; it is we who choose to yield to our burning desires, those forces aptly imaged as goddesses and gods. We are the battleground on which the gods war among themselves.

The ancients called them the gods; we call them emotional forces. For better or worse, our environment teaches us how to deal with these "gods" that operate in us. But like the sons and daughters of the House of Atreus, we too inherit the karma of our family in the form of emotionally-charged biases, prejudices, feuds, complexes, and energy patterns that we must recognize and retire if we are to be free to realize our innate potential.

Religious tradition, depth psychology, and mythology recognize this innate potential in various ways. In the Hindu tradition, for example, the term *atman* refers to the divine essence of the individual. According to this view, we are not primarily the physical body, the emotions, or our personality, but a fractal of the Transcendent Self, the Absolute, God.[3] The Christian tradition speaks of the *imitatio*

Christi, the imitation of Christ, which we can understand non-literally as fulfilling our God-given destiny. In this sense, imitating Christ would be to realize our spiritual gifts, our innate potential, and to accept the suffering involved in following our calling. Jungian depth psychology talks of realizing the self, which is a secular way of speaking about the same phenomenon: making real in the world, in some way, what each of us deep down feels is our essence, our fundamental nature, the fractal of the divine in each of us. The archetype of the hero's journey describes the first steps on the path that leads to realization of the self.

One of the most important tasks of education, psychoanalysis, and soul-work is initially to make conscious and eventually to free us from our unconscious attachment to our parents and identification with parents' unresolved complexes and unrealized potential. Family karma is the dragon that hoards the diamond of our selfhood. The goal of such an opus is for us as conscious adults to retain what is valuable and reject what is dross from the legacy of our family. In doing so, we have the opportunity to retire the curse and the suffering of our ancestors, and perpetuate their spiritual and creative lineage. This is a sacred task, a great burden, and a yet greater opportunity for each of us on the path to the soul. If we all undertake and complete this task, we can rid the collective consciousness and unconscious of the cumulative psychic toxicity of our ancestors' problems, and leave the planet a more conscious, better informed, and safer place to live.

Journal Exercise: How Things Look Now

1. As you now look at your grandparents' relationship, what similarities and/or differences do you recognize between their relationship and your intimate relationship(s)?

2. What new information have you discovered about how each of your grandparents react(ed) emotionally to various situations? Do you find yourself reacting in similar ways, even though your reactions don't make any sense to you?

3. How do you now understand dreams in which your father or mother, or grandfather or grandmother, does something noticeably out of character (i.e., differently than they act in waking life)?

4. If you have physical ailments that "run in the family" for which there appears to be no medical treatment, what hypotheses do you now have for understanding them?

5. What sort of work do you do? Who among your older relatives (parents, grandparents, aunts and uncles) does/did the same sort of work you do? What does/did your older relatives say about the line of work you are in? How do you feel about all of this now?

6. If you are an adopted child, how do you now understand the attitudes and behaviors you have that have no precedent in your adoptive family?

7. What do you now think about the "ancestral dramas" in your family line? (For example, "Men in this family always/never...." "Our family does...." "The women in our family...." "Children are supposed to....")

8. Having explored a lot of family territory in the course of reading this book and working through the Journal Exercises, how do you relate to, or what do you feel about, your family traditions? (For example, you like them; you rebel against them; they give you a sense of security; they stifle you; you believe you have to uphold them; etc.)

9. What additional functional as well as dysfunctional coping strategies that you share with other members of your (extended) family have you now identified?

(Functional coping strategies, for example, would be anticipating situations or consequences of actions; observing your emotions and behavior; being able to laugh rather than throw a tantrum. Dysfunctional coping strategies, for example, would be denial; blaming others; resorting to temper tantrums, excessive drinking, or gambling to manage stress.)

10. If you have been in counseling or psychotherapy, what issues have you worked on? How effective has your counseling or psychotherapy been in

resolving your issues of concern? What do you now believe you need to work on next?

THE COURAGE TO BECOME YOURSELF

It's sad to realize how many years we may have devoted to living unauthentically. Family karma can do that to us: subtly, or not so subtly, coercing us to live someone else's life. But before you can change that, you have to recognize that it is the life of another person: lived or not lived, their successes, their fears, their maladaptations. Once you start to get a lay of the family karma territory, you need to muster the courage to make the necessary changes.

Remember Lord Krishna's advice to Arjuna, his protégé, in the Bhagavad Gita (3:35): Your own soul path, even if you don't follow it perfectly, is better than someone else's soul path, even though you never miss a step. The longest journey begins with the first step. Regardless how old or how young you are, you can begin the task of releasing yourself from the karma of your family.

We invite and encourage you to take that first step, and the steps that follow upon it.

APPENDIX A:
ADDITIONAL READING

The books referenced are only a small selection from among the many useful resources. What we have listed are, of course, our favorites. We hope these few titles will further speed you on your journey.

CHAKRAS

Arewa, Caroline Shola. *Opening to Spirit: Contacting the Healing Power of the Chakras & Honoring African Spirituality*. London: Thorsons, 1998. A fine introduction to the chakras, including psychological, medical, mythological, and herbal information and exercises relating to each chakra.

Karagulla, Shafica, M.D., and Dora van Gelder Kunz. *The Chakras and the Human Energy Fields*. Wheaton: Quest Books/Theosophical Publishing House, 1989. Karagulla and van Gelder Kunz's work rests on solid medical diagnosis that correlates clairvoyant diagnosis. A must if you are especially interested in the medical aspects of chakra work.

Leadbeater, C. W. *The Chakras*. Wheaton: Quest Books/Theosophical Publishing House, 1927/1997. This is a classic, but probably not the first book to read on the chakras.

Simpson, Liz. *The Book of Chakra Healing*. New York: Sterling Publishing Co., 1999. Another good introduction with useful meditation and physical exercises for balancing and strengthening the chakras.

Wauters, Ambika. *Healing with the Energy of the Chakras*. Freedom, CA: Crossing Press, 1998. Yet another practical introduction and overview.

DREAMS

Bosnak, Robert. *A Little Course in Dreams: A Basic Handbook of Jungian Dreamwork.* Boston: Shambhala Publications, 1988. The subtitle says it all. Bosnak reviews all the essentials of Jungian dream work, with special attention to embodied re-experiencing of the dream.

Hall, James A. *Jungian Dream Interpretation: A Handbook of Theory and Practice.* Toronto: Inner City Books, 1983. Hall's book is a classic presentation. Very readable. Also has a handy glossary of Jungian terms.

GENOGRAM

McGoldrick, Monica, and Randy Gerson. *Genograms in Family Assessment.* New York: W. W. Norton & Company, 1985. McGoldrick and Gerson's text will lead you as deep into genogram construction as you want to go. Very useful, whether you are a beginner or an expert.

MORPHOGENIC FIELDS

Sheldrake, Rupert. *A New Science of Life: The Hypothesis of Formative Causation,* 2nd ed. London: Blond and Briggs, 1985. This is Sheldrake's classic presentation of his ideas on morphogenic fields.

———. *The Presence of the Past: Morphic Resonance and the Habits of Nature.* New York: Times Books, 1988.

———. *The Rebirth of Nature: The Greening of Science and God.* New York: Bantam, 1990.

———. *Dogs That Know When Their Owners Are Coming Home and Other Unexplained Powers of Animals.* New York: Crown Publishers, 1999.

Sheldrake, Rupert, and Matthew Fox. *Natural Grace: Dialogues on Creation, Darkness, and the Soul in Spirituality and Science.* New York: Doubleday, 1996.

APPENDIX B: GENEALOGY

Researching your genealogy involves several steps. The material we are presenting here is based on the excellent pamphlet, *Researching the Family Tree*,[1] prepared by the staff at the Milwaukee Public Library, and excerpted by kind permission.

GETTING STARTED

Interviewing members of your family is the place to start. Get all the information you can from relatives. Family photo albums and old family bibles can be great sources of information because they often contain names and dates.

Read at least one book on how to do genealogical research. Here are several you might consider:

Doane, Gilbert H. and James B. Bell. *Searching for Your Ancestors : The How and Why of Genealogy.* 6th ed. Minneapolis: University of Minnesota Press, 1992. This is a classic, and a good one for a start.

Croom, Emily Anne. *Unpuzzling Your Past: The Best-Selling Basic Guide to Genealogy.* 4th ed., expanded, updated, and revised. Cincinnati, Ohio: Betterway Books, 2001.

The Source: A Guidebook of American Genealogy. Loretto Dennis Szucs and Sandra Hargreaves Luebking, eds. Salt Lake City: Ancestry, 1997. This is a one of the two most complete compendia.

Printed Sources: A Guide to Published Genealogical Records. Kory L. Meyerink, ed. Salt Lake City, Utah: Ancestry, 1998. This is the other of the two most complete compendia.

On the Internet you can find a great deal of information on genealogy. One fine Web site is RootsWeb.com. Check out especially their

"Guide to Tracing Family Trees" where you will find many useful links for locating and tracing adoption records:

http://www.rootsweb.com/~rwguide/lesson31.html

DIGGING DEEPER

As you delve into your genealogy, you may find it useful or necessary to consult more specialized resources. This might include immigration and naturalization records:

Newman, John J. *American Naturalization Records, 1790–1990: What They Are and How to Use Them.* Bountiful, Utah: Heritage Quest, 1998.

Or studying family photographs:

Taylor, Maureen Alice. *Uncovering Your Ancestry through Family Photographs.* Cincinnati, Ohio: Betterway Books, 2000.

Ethnic and minority resources also abound:

Angus Baxter has written several volumes devoted to British, Irish, Canadian, European, and German roots.

Burrough, Tony. *Black Roots: A Beginner's Guide to Tracing the African American Family Tree.* New York: Fireside Book, 2001.

Smith, Franklin Carater and Emily Anne Croom. *A Genealogist's Guide to Discovering Your African-American Ancestors: How to Find and Record Your Unique Heritage.* Cincinnati, Ohio: Betterway Books, 2003

Woodtor, Dee Parmer. *Finding a Place Called Home: A Guide to African-American Genealogy and Historical Identity.* New York: Random House, 1999.

FURTHER RESEARCH

By now you are deep into your search. Consider consulting the various bibliographies and indices of genealogical records, passenger lists, the Library of Congress, and the National Archives. There are many published family histories where you might find useful information. Since

1790, the federal government has taken a census every 10 years. And the 1850 federal census is the first to list each person by name. Birth, death, and marriage records may be of help, and can be found in larger libraries and in state bureaus of vital records or state historical societies. Lastly, newspapers are a source worth researching for marriages, deaths, births, land transactions, and legal suits.

When searching the library for genealogical information, start with the library catalogue. Many public libraries now have their catalogue of holdings on line, so you can often work from home. The Milwaukee Public Library recommends that you "be as specific as possible when using search terms. The broader the search term, the longer it will take to get results. When in doubt, ask a reference librarian. They will love the attention."

This is only a sampling of possible resources. Your local library is always a good place to start, an Internet search will net you all sorts of hits. We wish you well in your exploration of your ancestry, and hope you will discover not only buried family curses and skeletons in the closet, but lost family blessings as well.

NOTES

Chapter 1

1. Ian Stevenson, *Twenty Cases Suggestive of Reincarnation* (University Press of Virginia, 1966), *Unlearned Language* (University Press of Virginia, 1984), *Children Who Remember Previous Lives* (University of Virginia Press, 1987).

2. Ian Stevenson, "Phobias in Children Who Claim to Remember Previous Lives," *Journal of Scientific Exploration*, vol. 4, no. 2 (from the abstract).

3. Ian Stevenson, "Unusual Play in Young Children Who Claim to Remember Past Lives, *Journal of Scientific Exploration*, vol. 14, no. 4 (from the abstract).

4. Ian Stevenson, "Birthmarks and Birth Defects Corresponding to Wounds on Deceased Persons," *Journal of Scientific Exploration*, vol. 7, no. 4 (from the abstract).

5. Ian Stevenson, "Birthmarks."

6. Stawant K. Pasricha, "Cases of the Reincarnation Type in Northern India with Birthmarks and Birth Defects," *Journal of Scientific Exploration*, vol. 12, no. 2 (from the abstract).

7. Interested readers will find a detailed discussion of the various aspects of dharma in Ashok Bedi, *The Path to the Soul* (York Beach, Maine: Samuel Weiser, 2000).

Chapter 3

1. Psalm 79: 6, 9.

2. Isaiah 65: 7.

3. Daniel 14:42.

4. Ronald Kessler, *The Sins of the Father: Joseph P. Kennedy and the Dynasty He Founded* (New York: Warner Books, 1996), pp. 284-286.

5. Kessler, *Sins*, pp. 312 ff.

6. Seymour M. Hersh, *The Dark Side of Camelot* (Boston, New York, Toronto: Little, Brown, 1997) p. 13.

7. See Kessler, *Sins*; also Barbara Gibson, *The Kennedys: The Third Generation* (New York: Thunder's Mouth, 1993); and Hersh, *Camelot*.

8. Hersh, *Camelot*, pp. 341-371.

9. Quoted in Hersh, *Camelot*, p. 288

10. Hersh, *Camelot*, p. 2.

11. Ronald Steel, Review of *Hostage to Fortune: The Letters of Joseph P. Kennedy*, edited by Amanda Smith, *The New York Review of Books* XLVIII, no. 16 (October 18, 2001): 31-39, 39.

12. Kessler, *Sins*, p. 5.

13. Shakespeare, *Julius Caesar*, II:I.

14. Steele, *Hostage*, p. 31.

15. See Kessler, *Sins*; Hersch, *Camelot*; Steel, *Hostage*.
16. Kessler, *Sins*, p. 3.
17. Kessler, *Sins*, p. 287 ff.
18. Kessler, *Sins*, p. 389.
19. Kessler, *Sins*, p. 23.

Chapter 4

1. Heinz Kohut, *The Restoration of the Self*, (New York: International Universities Press, 1977) and *How Does Analysis Cure*, A. Goldberg, P. Stepansky, eds. (Chicago: University of Chicago Press, 1984).
2. Kohut, *Restoration of the Self*.

Chapter 5

1. Carl G. Jung, "Introduction to Wickes's *The Inner World of Childhood*" (1927), in *The Development of Personality, The Collected Works of C. G. Jung*, vol. 17 (Princeton: Princeton University Press, 1970), ¶ 80, p. 39.
2. Jung, "Introduction to Wickes's," ¶ 84, p. 41.
3. C. G. Jung, "A Review of the Complex Theory" (1934), in *The Structure and Dynamics of the Psyche, The Colleted Works of C. G. Jung*, vol. 8 (Princeton: Princeton University Press, 1969), pp. 92–104. See also Jung, *Experimental Researches, The Collected Works of C. G. Jung*, vol. 2 (Princeton: Princeton University Press, 1973).
4. Jung, *Experimental Researches*, ¶ 1006 ff.
5. C. G. Jung, "The Family Constellation" (1909), in *Experimental Researches, The Collected Works of C. G. Jung*, vol. 2 (Princeton: Princeton University Press, 1973), ¶ 1005.
6. Rupert Sheldrake, *Dogs That Know When Their Owners Are Coming Home: And Other Unexplained Powers of Animals* (New York: Crown, 1999), pp. 301–318.
7. Jung, "The Family Constellation," ¶ 999–1014.
8. See Ashok Bedi, *Path to the Soul* (York Beach, ME: Samuel Weiser, 2000).
9. Caroline Shola Arewa, *Opening to Spirit* (London: Thorsons, 1998), p. 11.
10. Joseph Campbell, *The Mythic Image*, Bollingen Series C (Princeton: Princeton University Press, 1974), p. 341.
11. Campbell, *Mythic Image*, p. 3456.
12. Arewa, *Opening to Spirit*, p.143.
13. Campbell, *Mythic Image*, p. 350.
14. C. G. Jung, *The Psychology of Kundalini Yoga*, Sonu Shamdasani, ed., Bollingen Series XCIX (Princeton: Princeton University Press, 1996), p. 45.
15. Campbell, *Mythic Image*, p. 356.
16. Campbell, *Mythic Image*, p. 368.
17. Swami Adiswarananda, *Sri Ramakrisha Biography* (http://www.ramakrishna.org/: Ramakrishna-Vivekananda Center of New York, 1996).
18. Swami Yatiswarananda, "A Glimpse into Hindu Religious Symbology," in Sri Ramakrishna Centenary Committee, eds., *Cultural Heritage of India*, vol. II (Calcutta: Belur Math, 1937), cited in Joseph Campbell, *Mythic Image*, p. 380.

19. Arewa, *Opening to Spirit*, p. 239 f.
20. Campbell, *Mythic Image*, p. 381.

Chapter 6

1. C. G. Jung, *C. G. Jung Letters*, vol. 1, Gerhard Adler and Aniela Jaffé, eds., Bollingen Series XCV (Princeton: Princeton University Press, 1973), p. 234.
2. Maureen Alice Taylor, *All About Adoption Research* (http://www.RootsWeb.com-rwguide/lesson31.html), copyright 1998–2002 MyFamily.com Inc.
3. Jayne Askin, *Search: A Handbook for Adoptees and Birthparents*, 3rd edition (Westport, CT: Oryx Press, 1998). Quoted from http://www.RootsWeb.com-rwguide/lesson31.html. Copyright 1998–2002, MyFamily.com Inc.
4. Sigmund Freud's *Psychopathology of Everyday Life* (New York: Penguin USA, 2003) is a classic study of these more subtle complexes.
5. *Diagnostic and Statistical Manual of Mental Disorders*, 4th edition (Washigton, D.C.: American Psychiatric Association, 1994), p. 417 ff.

Chapter 8

1. "[T]he original pattern or model of which all things of the same type are representations or copies. . . ." *Merriam-Webster's Deluxe Dictionary*, 10th collegiate edition (New York: Merriam-Webster, Inc., 1998), p. 93. *Type*, from the Greek "*tupos*, a mark, an impression, caused by a blow or sharp stroke." Eric Partridge, *Origins: A Short Etymological Dictionary of Modern English* (New York: Greenhouse Press, 1983), p. 747.
2. "Fractal" comes from the Latin, *fractus* = broken, uneven. The term is used in chaos theory to refer to an irregularly shaped part whose irregularity conforms to the irregularity of the larger whole of which it is a part.
3. Subramuniyaswami, *Dancing with Siva: Hinduism's Contemporary Catechism* (Kappa, Hawaii: Himalayan Academy, 1993), p. 689.

Appendix B

1. *Researching the Family Tree with Genealogical Help from Your Milwaukee Public Library* (Milwaukee: Milwaukee Public Library, 1996).

BIBLIOGRAPHY

Adiswarananda, Swami. Sri Ramakrisha Biography.
　　http://www.ramakrishna.org: Ramakrishna-Vivekananda
　　Center of New York, 1996.
Arewa, Caroline Shola. *Opening to Spirit*. London: Thorsons, 1998.
Askin, Jayne. *Search: A Handbook for Adoptees and Birthparents*, 3rd edi-
　　tion. Westport, CT: Oryx Press, 1998.
Bedi, Ashok. *The Path to the Soul*. York Beach, ME: Samuel Weiser, 2000.
Campbell, Joseph. *The Mythic Image*. Bollingen Series C. Princeton:
　　Princeton University Press, 1974.
Diagnostic and Statistical Manual of Mental Disorders, 4th edition.
　　Washington, D.C.: American Psychiatric Association, 1994.
Freud, Sigmund. *The Psychopathology of Everyday Life*. New York:
　　Penguin USA, 2003.
Greene, Liz, and Howard Sasportas. *The Development of the Personality*.
　　York Beach, ME: Samuel Weiser, 1987.
Gibson, Barbara. *The Kennedys: The Third Generation*. New York:
　　Thunder's Mouth Press, 1993.
Goldberg, A. and P. Stepansky, eds. *How Does Analysis Cure*. Chicago:
　　University of Chicago Press, 1984.
Hersh, Seymour M. *The Dark Side of Camelot*. Boston, New York,
　　Toronto: Little, Brown, 1997.
The Jerusalem Bible. Garden City: Doubleday & Company, 1966.
Jung, C. G. *C. G. Jung Letters*, vol. 1. Gerhard Adler and Aneila Jaffé,
　　eds. Bollingen Series XCV. Princeton: Princeton University
　　Press, 1973.
————. "The Family Constellation" (1909). In *Experimental
　　Researches, The Collected Works of C. G. Jung*, vol. 2. R. F. C.

Hull, trans. Bollingen Series XX. Princeton: Princeton University Press, 1973.

———. "Introduction to Wickes's *The Inner World of Childhood*" (1927). In *The Development of Personality, The Collected Works of C. G. Jung*, vol. 17. R.F.C. Hull, trans. Bollingen Series XX. Princeton: Princeton University Press, 1970.

———. *The Psychology of Kundalini Yoga.* Sonu Shamdasani, ed. Bollingen Series XCIX. Princeton: Princeton University Press, 1996.

———. "A Review of the Complex Theory" (1934). In *The Structure and Dynamics of the Psyche, The Colleted Works of C. G. Jung*, vol. 8. R. F. C. Hull, trans. Bollingen Series XX. Princeton: Princeton University Press, 1969.

Kessler, Ronald. *The Sins of the Father: Joseph P. Kennedy and the Dynasty He Founded.* New York: Warner Books, 1996.

Kohut, Heinz. *The Restoration of the Self.* New York: International Universities Press, 1977.

Leamer, Lawrence. *The Kennedy Men.* New York: Morrow, 2001.

Merriam-Webster's Deluxe Dictionary. 10th collegiate edition. New York: Merriam-Webster, Inc., 1998.

Partridge, Eric. *Origins: A Short Etymological Dictionary of Modern English.* New York: Greenwich House, 1983.

Pasricha, Stawant K. "Cases of the Reincarnation Type in Northern India with Birthmarks and Birth Defects," *Journal of Scientific Exploration* 12, no. 2 (from the abstract).

Researching the Family Tree with Genealogical Help from Your Milwaukee Public Library. Milwaukee: Milwaukee Public Library, 1996.

Sheldrake, Rupert. *Dogs That Know When Their Owners Are Coming Home: And Other Unexplained Powers of Animals.* New York: Crown Publishers, 1999.

Steele, Ronald. Review of *Hostage to Fortune: The Letters of Joseph P. Kennedy.* Amanda Smith, ed. *The New York Review of Books* XLVIII, no. 16 (October 18, 2001): 31-39.

Stevenson, Ian. "Birthmarks and Birth Defects Corresponding to Wounds on Deceased Persons," *Journal of Scientific Exploration* 7, no. 4.

———. *Children Who Remember Previous Lives*. University of Virginia Press, 1987.

———. "Phobias in Children Who Claim to Remember Previous Lives," *Journal of Scientific Exploration* 4, no. 2.

———. *Unlearned Language*. University Press of Virginia, 1984.

———. "Unusual Play in Young Children Who Claim to Remember Past Lives," *Journal of Scientific Exploration* 14, no. 4.

———. *Twenty Cases Suggestive of Reincarnation*. University Press of Virginia, 1966.

Subramuniyaswami. *Dancing with Siva: Hinduism's Contemporary Catechism*. Kappa, Hawaii: Himalayan Academy, 1993.

Taylor, Maureen Alice. *All About Adoption Research* (http://www.RootsWeb.com-rwguide/lesson31.html: MyFamily.com Inc., 1998–2002.

Yatiswarananda, Swami. "A Glimpse into Hindu Religious Symbology." In Sri Ramakrishna Centenary Committee, eds. *Cultural Heritage of India*, II. 3 vols. Calcutta: Belur Math, 1937.

INDEX